James

New International Biblical Commentary

James

Peter H. Davids

New Testament Editor,
W. Ward Gasque

HENDRICKSON
PUBLISHERS
PEABODY, MASSACHUSETTS 01961-3473

To Arnim Riemenschneider
Principal (Schulleiter) of the Bibelschule Wiedenest
Bergneustadt, Germany
In thankfulness for friendship and example

No one I know better lived before me the
virtues of the Epistle of James, especially prayer,
generosity, holiness, and the control of the tongue.

Table of Contents

Foreword
New International Biblical Commentary

Although it does not appear on the standard best-seller lists, the Bible continues to outsell all other books. And in spite of growing secularism in the West, there are no signs that interest in its message is abating. Quite to the contrary, more and more men and women are turning to its pages for insight and guidance in the midst of the ever-increasing complexity of modern life.

This renewed interest in Scripture is found both outside and inside the church. It is found among people in Asia and Africa as well as in Europe and North America; indeed, as one moves outside of the traditionally Christian countries, interest in the Bible seems to quicken. Believers associated with the traditional Catholic and Protestant churches manifest the same eagerness for the Word that is found in the newer evangelical churches and fellowships.

We wish to encourage and, indeed, strengthen this worldwide movement of lay Bible study by offering this new commentary series. Although we hope that pastors and teachers will find these volumes helpful in both understanding and communicating the Word of God, we do not write primarily for them. Our aim is to provide for the benefit of every Bible reader reliable guides to the books of the Bible—representing the best of contemporary scholarship presented in a form that does not require formal theological education to understand.

The conviction of editor and authors alike is that the Bible belongs to the people and not merely to the academy. The message of the Bible is too important to be locked up in erudite and esoteric essays and monographs written only for the eyes of theological specialists. Although exact scholarship has its place in the service of Christ, those who share in the teaching office of the church have a responsibility to make the results of their research accessible to the Christian community at large. Thus, the Bible scholars who join in the presentation of this series write with these broader concerns in view.

A wide range of modern translations is available to the contemporary Bible student. Most of them are very good and much to be preferred—for understanding, if not always for beauty—to the older King James Version (the so-called Authorized Version of the Bible). The Revised Standard Version has become the standard English translation in many seminaries and colleges and represents the best of modern Protestant scholarship. It is also available in a slightly altered "common Bible" edition with the Catholic imprimatur, and a third revised edition is due out shortly. In addition, the New American Bible is a fresh translation that represents the best of post-Vatican II Roman Catholic biblical scholarship and is in a more contemporary idiom than that of the RSV.

The New Jerusalem Bible, based on the work of French Catholic scholars but vividly rendered into English by a team of British translators, is perhaps the most literary of the recent translations, while the New English Bible is a monument to modern British Protestant research. The Good News Bible is probably the most accessible translation for the person who has little exposure to the Christian tradition or who speaks and reads English as a second language. Each of these is, in its own way, excellent and will be consulted with profit by the serious student of Scripture. Perhaps most will wish to have several versions to read, both for variety and for clarity of understanding—though it should be pointed out that no one of them is by any means flawless or to be received as the last word on any given point. Otherwise, there would be no need for a commentary series like this one!

We have chosen to use the New International Version as the basis for this series, not because it is necessarily the best translation available but because it is becoming increasingly used by lay Bible students and pastors. It is the product of an international team of "evangelical" Bible scholars who have sought to translate the Hebrew and Greek documents of the original into "clear and natural English . . . idiomatic [and] . . . contemporary but not dated," suitable for "young and old, highly educated and less well educated, ministers and laymen [sic]." As the translators themselves confess in their preface, this version is not perfect. However, it is as good as any of the others mentioned above and more popular than most of them.

Each volume will contain an introductory chapter detailing the background of the book and its author, important themes, and other helpful information. Then, each section of the book will be expounded as a whole, accompanied by a series of notes on items in the text that need further clarification or more detailed explanation. Appended to the end of each volume will be a bibliographical guide for further study.

Our new series is offered with the prayer that it may be an instrument of authentic renewal and advancement in the worldwide Christian community and a means of commending the faith of the people who lived in biblical times and of those who seek to live by the Bible today.

W. WARD GASQUE
E. Marshall Sheppard Professor of Biblical Studies
Regent College, Vancouver, BC, Canada

Acknowledgments

First, I wish to thank Professor W. Ward Gasque for inviting me to write this commentary and editing it, and Wm. B. Eerdmans Publishing Company for raising no objection to my doing a popular version of my commentary on the Greek text of James published by them (*The Epistle of James,* New International Greek Testament Commentary Series, 1982). This has given me the chance to explain what was said in that commentary in a concrete and practical way for those who do not read Greek. The notes in this work are in some ways abbreviations of those in the other, but in other ways they go beyond the other work in citing practical works of pastoral helpfulness. There is a lot of overlap (after all, the same scholar wrote, using mostly the same notes and books, on the same New Testament book), yet this is a different work with a new audience and purpose constantly in mind. Those who mistake its purpose for that of the other book will be disappointed, and vice versa. I hope that each will be appreciated for what it is and intends to do.

As is every work, this book is a communal project. I have dedicated it to Arnim Riemenschneider, who was Studienleiter of Bibelschule Wiedenest when I taught there (1974–76) and is now Schulleiter (Principal, or Dean). It was there that I wrote my first published articles (for *New Testament Studies* and *The Illustrated Bible Dictionary*). More importantly, it was there that I learned to love at an emotional level the German Anabaptist/Pietist tradition for which living the gospel is so important. It is this form of the Plymouth Brethren movement (the base of Wiedenest's evangelical alliance mentality) to which I joyfully subscribe. I learned much of this not from books but by having it lived before me. I have tried in this book to express some of what I learned.

I am thankful to Harper & Row for initially taking on this commentary in their Good News Commentary series and their care in doing the original copy editing. They assisted me in gaining a sense of how to write with inclusive language. I am even more thankful to Hendrickson Publishers for shifting this commentary to the New International Version, editing it carefully, and giving me a chance to revise it and present it to the wider audience for which it was designed.

Further thanks go to Trinity Episcopal School for Ministry for granting me sabbatical leave for the year 1982–83, which gave me the time to write, and to New College for Advanced Christian Studies, Berkeley, for giving me a place to live and write. Most of this work was written in their library. Pauline Odom, assistant to the treasurer, laboriously typed my handwritten manuscript and deserves the credit for its readability. This revised version owes thanks to classes at Regent College, Vancouver, who assisted me in continuing to work through James material, and especially to Austin Avenue Chapel, Coquitlam, BC, which employed me, knowing full well that much of my time would go towards writing. Few churches are this tolerant and far-sighted.

Further thanks goes to Dr. Ronald Youngblood, editor of the *Journal of the Evangelical Theological Society*, for permission to use an edited version of an article, "Theological Perspectives on the Epistle of James," originally published by that journal (vol. 23 [1980], pp. 97–104) as the thematic emphases section in the Introduction. To my wife and family belong thanks for suffering through yet another book, not once but twice. My hope is that this book will help many in single-hearted devotion to Christ, which is both James' goal and mine.

Abbreviations

AB	Anchor Bible
AnBib	Analecta Biblica
APOT	*Apocrypha and Pseudepigrapha of the Old Testament*, edited by R. H. Charles (Oxford: Clarendon Press, 1913)
ATR	*Anglican Theological Review*
b.	Babylonian Talmud
Bib	*Biblica*
BJRL	*Bulletin of the John Rylands Library*
CBQ	*Catholic Biblical Quarterly*
ConB	Coniectanea Biblica
Dead Sea Scrolls	
1 QS	The Rule of the Community
1 QH	The Thanksgiving Hymns
1 QM	The War of the Sons of Light with the Sons of Darkness
CD	Cairo Damascus Document
11 Q Ps^a	Psalms Scroll from cave 11
EvQ	*The Evangelical Quarterly*
Ex	*The Expositor*
ExpTim	*The Expository Times*
GNB	Good News Bible
Hermas	The Shepherd of Hermas (Apostolic Fathers)
HNTC	Harper's New Testament Commentary
HTR	*Harvard Theological Review*
HUCA	*Hebrew Union College Annual*
ICC	International Critical Commentary
IEJ	*Israel Exploration Journal*
Int	*Interpretation*
JAAR	*Journal of the American Academy of Religion*
JBL	*Journal of Biblical Literature*
JQR	*Jewish Quarterly Review*
JSS	*Journal of Semitic Studies*

JTS	*Journal of Theological Studies*
m.	Mishnah
MNTC	Moffatt New Testament Commentary
NIDNTT	*New International Dictionary of New Testament Theology,* edited by C. Brown (Grand Rapids: Zondervan, 1975–1978)
NIGTC	New International Greek Testament Commentary
NIV	New International Version
NLCNT	New London Commentary on the New Testament
NovT	*Novum Testamentum*
NovTSup	Supplements to *Novum Testamentum*
NTS	*New Testament Studies*
R.	Rabbi
RevExp	*Review and Expositor*
RSV	Revised Standard Version
SB	*Studia Biblica*
SBT	Studies in Biblical Theology
SE	*Studia Evangelica*
SJT	*Scottish Journal of Theology*
SP	*Studia Patristica*
ST	*Studia Theologica*
StBTh	*Studia Biblica et Theologica*
SWJT	*Southwestern Journal of Theology*
t.	Tosefta
TDNT	*Theological Dictionary of the New Testament,* edited by G. Kittel and G. Frederick (Grand Rapids: Wm. B. Eerdmans, 1964–1976)
Th.	*Themelios*
TNTC	Tyndale New Testament Commentary
TU	*Texte und Untersuchungen*
Tyn.B.	*Tyndale Bulletin*
VE	*Vox Evangelica*
VTSup	Supplements to *Vetus Testamentum*
ZAW	*Zeitschrift für alttestamentliche Wissenschaft*
ZNW	*Zeitschrift für neutestamentliche Wissenschaft*

Commentaries on James are referred to by author and *James*, e.g., S. S. Law, *James*. Full details are in "For Further Reading."

Scripture quotations are from the New International Version or are the author's translation unless otherwise noted.

Quotations from the Apostolic Fathers are from J. Sparks, *The Apostolic Fathers* (Nashville: Thomas Nelson, 1978).

Quotations from the Apocrypha are from the RSV unless otherwise noted.

Quotations from the Pseudepigrapha (including m. *Aboth*) are from *APOT*.

Introduction

The Epistle of James is one of the most exciting parts of the New Testament. It has a hard-hitting punch and a reality-oriented attitude that catch readers unaware and astound them, while also offering them practical guidelines for life. Yet at the same time, it has been a neglected book, for ever since Luther called it an epistle of straw lacking the wheat of the gospel (which for him was Paul as Luther understood him), Protestants in general have struggled with the work. The result has been that the work has been pushed aside, so that it is only in the last two decades that a significant number of commentaries and studies on James have begun to appear. One now sees that the ugly duckling is indeed a swan, the neglected stepchild the true heir, for nowhere does the voice of Jesus speak to the church more clearly than in James. As the commentary progresses, the reader will see that James is an example of how the early church believers used and applied the words of Jesus to their daily life.

Authorship

The first issue to address in any study of a New Testament book is that of authorship. The straightforward claim of the work is rather clear: "James, a servant of God and of the Lord Jesus Christ" (1:1). The scripture knows of several Jameses or Jacobs (the Hebrew for which *James* is the Greek), but most can be quickly eliminated. A few scholars have argued that the work is claiming to be by Jacob the son of Isaac, and that it allegorically presents the names of his wives and sons. There is literature of this type (e.g., the *Testaments of the Twelve Patriarchs*) written about the same time as the New Testament, but if James is an allegory it is not at all like the Testaments. Also, James is far too thoroughly Christian to be a Jewish work. So this "James" can be quickly passed over.

Then there is James son of Zebedee, brother of John. He was part of the inner circle of apostles around Jesus, so he knew him well enough to have used his sayings freely. Since James was a fisherman, it is hard to tell what kind of education he had, but he could certainly speak Greek, the original language of the epistle. Yet he probably did not live long enough to write the work, for sometime between A.D. 41 and 44, only eight to ten years after Jesus' resurrection and before any New Testament literature was written or Paul began his missionary journeys, Herod Agrippa I had this James executed "by the sword" (Acts 12:1-2). His short career and sudden end make him an unlikely candidate for author of this epistle.

The other James among the twelve disciples is James son of Alphaeus (Matt. 10:3), who is probably the same as James the Little (Mark 15:40). So little is known about this person that no one can say he absolutely could not have written the epistle, but it is unlikely. Could such a relative "unknown" have written the simple beginning of the letter? Would he not have felt a need to identify himself more clearly, especially since the letter is so weighty and authoritative? Again, the reader must reject this "James."

Martin Luther believed an otherwise unknown James wrote the work late in the first century. If one believes that the work was written so late, this hypothesis might be attractive, for James or Jacob was a common name among Jews and Jewish Christians. But again there are problems. Why would such a James not identify himself more fully? Is he trying to impersonate an earlier, better-known James? Why does he believe he has this much authority? The conclusion must be that this theory was simply Luther's attempt to ascribe the book to a person who lacked apostolic authority.

Finally, having rejected the other candidates, one has narrowed the field to James brother of Jesus, called the Just. This younger brother of Jesus must have known his older brother and his teaching well. However, he did not believe him during his lifetime (John 7:2-5), and he (probably along with Mary) helped try to take Jesus home "for his own good" (Mark 3:20-21, 31-35). After the resurrection James suddenly appears with Jesus' other brothers among the disciples in the upper room, praying for the Spirit (Acts 1:14). It is Paul who gives the reason for this "about-face": Jesus appeared to James after the resurrection before he appeared to the large apostolic company, and like the appearance to Paul, this was probably a converting experience (1 Cor. 15:7).

After his conversion, James' career in the church began. When the Twelve began to travel, after the stoning of Stephen, it is James who remained in Jerusalem. He is probably the James named first in Galatians 2:9 as approving Paul's mission (whom Paul calls an apostle in Gal. 1:19). He appears sending out church delegates in Galatians 2:12, he presides over the apostolic council in Acts 15 (and since his word is spoken last, it indicates that he had a higher status than Peter), and he receives and advises Paul with his collection in Acts 21. It is clear that James was the undisputed leader of the Jerusalem church and arguably the most influential Christian leader of his day. He remained in this position until shortly after Paul's arrest (A.D. 57).

In A.D. 62, three years after sending Paul to Rome, the procurator Festus died in office. During the period before the appointment and arrival of the procurator Albinus, the high priest Annas the Younger seized his chance and arraigned James and some others on the charge of having broken the Law. James was condemned and stoned. Although another member of the holy family, Symeon, was later chosen to succeed him, no leader equaled James in stature. The Jewish-Christian church in Jerusalem itself soon came to an end, for it fled to Pella in fear of the advancing Roman armies in A.D. 66 and was never afterward able to continue its mission to the Jews.

This James, a powerful and well-known figure of the early church, is surely the person indicated in the opening verse. He alone had the authority for a letter of this tone. He alone would be recognized by the mere mention of his name (so much so that Jude says "Jude, the brother of James" in Jude 1). The opening verses certainly intend to put his authority behind the epistle. The question that has been asked, however, is whether he truly stands there or whether the epistle is simply ascribed to him, much as the apocryphal work 1 Enoch (a Jewish work of the first century) was ascribed to Enoch, or Psalms of Solomon (a set of poems written by a Pharisee in the century before Christ) to Solomon.

Several points have been argued against James' authorship. First, the Greek of the letter is too good. Though this fact hardly comes out in English translation, the Greek of James is among the two or three best Greek styles in the New Testament, being full of catchwords, alliteration, and other points of beauty. All scholars admit that a Galilean carpenter's son would probably speak some Greek, but many ask, would its quality equal this standard of excellence, especially since James the Just remained in Jerusalem, the center of Aramaic-speaking Judaism, most of his life? Those who believe he could not have written such Greek argue a later author wrote the work in James' name.

Second, there are some philosophical phrases (e.g., "the whole course of his life" in 3:6) and other indications (e.g., all the quotations agree with the Greek Old Testament; none are distinctively Hebrew) that the author is very familiar with the Greek world. James the Just may well have spoken Greek, but would he, like this author, have known Greek philosophical ideas and been familiar with Sirach and Wisdom of Solomon (Jewish wisdom literature from the two centuries before Christ)? Would he not have quoted the Hebrew Old Testament? Furthermore, the epistle contains little of the Jewish legalism and ritualism that many connect with James the Just. Does this not show the work of a later author whose Judaism was that of the Greek Diaspora at best, or even that of a God-fearing Gentile?

Third, the Epistle of James is very similar to the Shepherd of Hermas, a late first-century Christian work written in Rome. It also shows similarities to 1 Peter (although there was no borrowing, just mutual use of a common tradition), which itself is often dated late in the first century. Does this not mean that James belongs there as well? After all, his church seems settled and struggling with problems of acculturation (e.g., acceptance of the rich), not the problems of a new, expanding, evangelistic community. Several scholars thus propose a life-setting in Rome at the end of the first century, which would rule out authorship by James the Just.

Finally, there is the relationship of James to Paul. A comparison of James 2:24 with Romans 3:20; 3:28; and 4:16 makes it appear that James is directly contradicting Paul. James uses Abraham as his chief example and cites Genesis 15:6 (in 2:23) as Paul does. That means that James must have been written after Paul coined his slogans, or even after Romans was written. James does not seem to understand the slogans, so perhaps he has heard them secondhand from someone who had read Romans but was misusing it. Now James the Just was present at the Jerusalem Council (Acts 15) where all these issues were argued face to face. Surely he would have understood Paul and would not have relied on secondhand data. But the epistle has the marks of being written after the controversy had died down, toward the late first century, long after James lay in the grave.

The arguments are powerful and have convinced many, but they are far from the whole story. On the matter of James and Paul, the commentary on 2:14–26 will show that they use terms differently. Paul has his own meanings for words, whereas James uses words in their older, Jewish sense (which is the reason the commentary will frequently cite extracanonical Jewish writings. It is quite possible James misunderstood Paul, but that was more likely earlier than later. In the period of Paul's first missionary journey, someone like John Mark may have brought a garbled version of Paul's teaching to Jerusalem. If James 2:14–26 is James' response to Paul before Paul explained what his position really was, it is possible James suggested the Abraham example to Paul— if Paul did not come by it quite independently. (In Gal. 4:21–31, Paul is probably borrowing an allegory from his opponents and turning it against them; he was quite capable of doing the same with those who misused James' arguments.) At the least, with such differences from Paul, James was more likely written before Romans rather than afterward when Paul's position was clearly known, for the real Paul would have agreed with what James meant even if he would have expressed it differently.

When it comes to James and the Shepherd of Hermas (a first-century Christian writer in Rome), it is clearly Hermas who is borrowing from James. By the time Hermas was written, copies of James had reached Rome; the epistle was used by Hermas, but he lacked James' Jewish background and so softened his condemnation of the rich and misunderstood several phrases (like James' teaching on prayer). This is hardly evidence that James was written at the same time as Hermas. Likewise, the relationship to 1 Peter depends on how long the tradition they both used lasted (it lasted at least until 1 Clement, a letter from the Roman church leader Clement to Corinth, was written in A.D. 96), when 1 Peter was written, and how early the tradition began.

The lack of "Jewishness" in the Epistle of James is only apparent. The phrases that appear philosophical may have originally come from a philosophical source, but they are used in very unphilosophical ways, for they have become the common expressions of the culture. The citations of the Old Testament may or may not come from the Greek Bible; in these five texts the Greek and Hebrew versions are identical. Furthermore Sirach and Wisdom of Solomon (both in the Apocrypha, i.e., Jewish works not accepted by Protestants as scripture) were widely read in Palestine, so the "Greek" culture of James would have been very much at home in Jerusalem. The truth is that one can picture a perfectly good Palestinian milieu for James. Most of the epistle's "Greekness" is only a surface appearance.

James the Just, contrary to popular opinion, was no legalist. Only two pieces of information would point in that direction. In the first (Gal. 2:12), "certain men [who] came from James" begin the Judaizing controversy. The text does not indicate whether James shared their views, but just states that he had sent them and thus they had enough authority to cause a disturbance, even if the purpose for which he sent them was very different. The second piece of information is a tradition from Hegesippus (an early Christian historian recorded by Eusebius) that portrays James the Just as a legal rigorist. Yet the tradition is not believable, for among other improbabilities, it has him entering the holy of holies in the temple. Most likely Hegesippus simply states as history what was in fact a theological description of James the Just.[1] As a basis for his historical character it is poor indeed, especially since Galatians 1:19 and 2:9 present him as accepting Paul and approving his mission, and Acts 15 and 21 present him as a mediating figure who holds the church together in unity by creating compromises between Paul and the rigorists. It is the picture in Acts that is in harmony with the Epistle of James.

Thus one returns to the quality of the Greek as the strongest argument against James the Just's authorship. This brings up another aspect of the epistle. It appears disjointed, but the same themes crop up in different words throughout the epistle. Indeed, there is a pattern to their appearance that F. O. Francis discovered fits a common pattern in literary epistles.[2] How can one account for an overall pattern that shows some inconsistency in vocabulary between parts (e.g., 1:13–15 and 4:1–3 or 1:2–4; 1:12; and 5:7–11)? Then there is the fact that even with the good Greek there are a number of awkward phrases that show a Semitic thought pattern (e.g., 2:1, or the "doer of the word"—NIV, "do what it says"—of 1:22). This seems strange, for if a person could use the high-quality Greek of this epistle, one would expect him to be able to avoid Semitisms, and a person who thought so Semitically could most likely not produce the Greek style of the epistle.

The solution to this dilemma is a more careful look at the work. It is clearly oral discourse, like the Greek diatribe, the synagogue homily, or a sermon. There are a number of connected discourses (2:1–13; 2:14–26; 3:1–12; etc.) plus a scattering of shorter sayings (e.g., 3:18; 4:17). Since these are usually on ethics, they are sometimes termed paraenesis, or ethical instruction. These pieces have been combined into an overall structure so that they fit together yet have not entirely lost their original separate character. That is the answer to the riddle. James the Just is probably the main source of the sayings and discourses, but he delivered his sermons in Aramaic or relatively Semitic Greek. Later, either because visitors to Jerusalem requested it, or because James' martyrdom stimulated it, the sermons of James were collected, edited into a book around his favorite themes, and circulated as a general letter. The editor improved the Greek, but acted conservatively so as not to obscure James' voice. This explanation appears to satisfy all the data. The letter is by James, but just as Paul used secretaries to write his epistles and they had a good deal of freedom, and Luke improves the Greek of sayings of Jesus (when compared to Mark or Matthew), so James had an editor—either a trusted colleague, or a leader of the church after his death— who preserved his teaching for future generations.

Form

The form or structure of the Epistle of James, as discovered by F. O. Francis[3] and later modified and developed by myself, is that of a literary letter (a letter designed to be published rather than mailed to real addressees) with a doubled opening. It has always been recognized that 1 John 1:2 repeats and extends 1:1.

Similarly, James 1:2–11 has three sections repeated and extended in 1:12–25. The same three topics appear in reverse order in 2:1–26, 3:1–4:12, and 4:13–5:6. There is a conclusion (5:7–11) and a closing (5:12–20). The closing covers three topics normally discussed in a Greek letter: oaths (5:12), health (5:13–18), and the reason for writing (5:19–20). The result is the following structure (using headings from the NIV, where they exist, for convenience, although in some cases we will subdivide them or limit their scope)

I. Greeting 1:1

II. Opening Statement (Trials and Temptations) 1:2–27
  1. Part 1
    1:2–8
    a. Testing 1:2–4
    b. Faith and Wisdom 1:5–8
    c. Poverty and Riches 1:9–11
  2. Part 2
    1:12–18
    a. Testing 1:12–15
    b. Life and the Tongue 1:16–18
    c. Listening and Doing 1:19–27
      (vv. 26–27 are transition and linking verses; vv. 19–21 belong with 16–18 as much as with 22–27)

III. Poverty and Riches 2:1–26
  1. Favoritism Forbidden 2:1–13
  2. Faith and Deeds 2:14–26

IV. Wisdom and the Tongue 3:1–4:12
  1. Taming the Tongue 3:1–12
  2. Two Kinds of Wisdom 3:13–18
  3. Submit Yourselves to God 4:1–10
  4. Warning against Judging a Christian Brother 4:11–12

V. Testing, Faith, and Wealth 4:13–5:6
  1. Boasting About Tomorrow 4:13–17
  2. Warning to Rich Oppressors 5:1–6

VI. Patience and Prayer = Closing 5:7–20
  1. Conclusion: Patience in Suffering 5:7–11
  2. Oaths 5:12
  3. The Prayer of Faith 5:13–18
  4. Purpose 5:19–20

Date

Given what was said earlier about the authorship and form of the epistle, its date can now be determined. Those, of course, who do not believe James the Just wrote the epistle at all date it relatively late, A.D. 70–130, most frequently A.D. 80–100. But it was argued earlier that James the Just *is* the source of the sermons contained in the epistle, which means that the source materials date from his lifetime; that is, before A.D. 62. Furthermore, James 2:14–26 was probably composed as a unit before James had a chance to discuss Paul's distinctive doctrines with him. That puts at least this part before A.D. 49. But this date is satisfactory for any of the epistle, for the church was by that time more than fifteen years old, which is fully old enough to have any of the problems described in James. Indeed, the decade of the 40s was a time of economic need in Jerusalem, which fits the kinds of economic insecurity and vulnerability that James' church is experiencing. Thus it is likely that much of the material in the epistle stems from the mid-40s and circulated orally or in rough Greek translations for a decade or so before being put in final form.

The second stage of the work, the final edited version, is harder to date. It is probably earlier than A.D. 66, for the flight of the church to Pella would have ended the continuity with Jerusalem and James the Just needed to collect a tradition. How much earlier is hard to determine. Most likely the death of James triggered the writing of the epistle, for with the living voice silent, there would surely have been a desire on the part of the grieving church to preserve his teaching to the true Israel, "to all God's people scattered over the whole world." This would also explain two other facts: (1) how Hermas got a copy in Rome by A.D. 96, for there was plenty of time between A.D. 66 and 96 for a copy to get to Jewish Christians there, and (2) why James is not used otherwise until Origen cites it about A.D. 256, for a Jewish-Christian work that was not useful in doctrinal controversy was surely half-forgotten with the Jerusalem church first in exile and then struggling for its distinctive existence as the Jewish mission collapsed with the fall of Jerusalem in A.D. 70.

Historical Background

The discussion of dating has already suggested a historical background, but it now remains to paint it in some detail. James' church lived in Jerusalem about fifteen years after the resurrection. Actually it was a series of house churches or Christian synagogues, each one having no more than about sixty members; most were far smaller, twenty to forty members. They met for worship, probably a modified form of the synagogue liturgy, and then celebrated the Lord's Supper immediately afterward. They also enjoyed the celebration of Jewish festivals and the temple services, as Acts shows. Each house church was directed by one or more elders; the elders as a group, presided over by James, ran the whole church. There were also deacons (as in Acts 6), whose job it was to collect charitable contributions and distribute them to the poorer members of the church.

There were many poor members, for as a whole, the church itself was poor. There were a number of reasons for this. First, there were many members from outside Jerusalem who could not ply their trade in the city (e.g., Peter and Andrew were fishermen). Some of these were pilgrims who had been converted at a festival time and had chosen not to go home, where there was no church to nurture them. Second, there were streams of visitors who wanted to learn about Christianity at the fountainhead, so to speak. These had to be fed, housed, even clothed, as hospitality was an important church function (see the Didache for how this worked later in the century).

Third, Christianity always tended to appeal to poor and oppressed folk: prostitutes, thieves, tax collectors, and the like were all attracted by the promise of forgiveness; the wealthy and powerful, though, saw a group of people with whom they would rather not associate. The poor heard a message of faith, hope, and justice (Jesus will return); it is they whom James calls "rich in faith" (2:5). Fourth, many older folk came to Jerusalem to die. When they heard of the resurrection in Jesus and were converted, they came under the care of the church. It would not be surprising that in some cases children who had been supporting them used the conversion as a welcome excuse to discontinue support. One wonders as well what happened to the livelihood of the "large number of priests" who believed (Acts 6:7). Fifth, Jerusalem itself fell on hard times. The city was in an economically marginal area, chosen for political and defensive rather than economic reasons. In the 40s there was a series of famines that required the help of wealthy aristocrats outside Palestine who sent food to the starving Jews of Jerusalem. The church suffered with the rest of the people but probably got little of the general relief.

Finally, there was persecution. The persecution in Jerusalem was rarely violent, but the Christians were a despised sect. This was especially true later when they refused to join the patriotic effort to free Palestine. Persecution could (and can) be very subtle: a laborer known as a Christian would be the last to be hired and would be the first fired when the economy slowed down. If a Christian were cheated out of wages or other rights by a Jewish leader, the mere fact he or she was a Christian would prejudice the case against the person wronged. None of this helped the church become rich.

The times were tumultuous. Herod Agrippa I, who had been a good king, died suddenly in A.D. 44 after a reign of only four years. He was followed by a series of venial procurators. Only the short-lived Festus was a decent ruler. They were open to graft and bribes of every sort and despised the Jews. Under them the Zealots arose as a "Palestine Liberation Front" and began attacking Romans and Roman sympathizers: banditry, coercion, and kidnappings for ransom became common news. The Roman proconsul often released Zealots when properly bribed with money stolen from Roman sympathizers.

The temple was in no better condition. The highpriestly families struggled for control of the office; every couple of years the high priest was changed. Many of the Jews felt the whole group of them was illegitimate to begin with, for they were not descendants of Zadok (1 Sam. 2:27-36; 2 Sam. 15:24-29; 1 Kings 2:26-27; 4:2—the last high priest of this line was killed in 170 B.C.). The lower clergy were oppressed and discriminated against by the greater priestly families, while the more powerful priestly clans were known for luxury, oppression of the poor, gossip, and intrigue. They were hardly spiritual leaders, but they were economically powerful.

Economically there were five groups in the land. On the bottom were slaves, who were not numerous in Palestine (in contrast to the rest of the empire) because Jewish law made them less profitable than hired workers (because if the slave converted, he or she had to be freed in the sabbatical year). Then came two groups of peasants. The poorer group were landless people who hired themselves out for the day; when there was no work, they starved. The less-poor group were farmers and artisans. The farmers owned their own farms, if they were lucky, but many had been forced by hard times to sell their farms to the wealthy and now worked as tenants and sharecroppers on land their family once owned. The next group up were merchants and traders, who as a whole were upwardly mobile. Some of them were rich; others only had enough. Since Jerusalem was not a trade center, they usually had to travel to pursue their business, unless they were part of the temple trade. But many could afford to live in Jerusalem part of the time. At the top of society were the large landowners, including the great priestly clans. They had large, tenant-farmed estates and so could spend time in Jerusalem enjoying their revenues and running the nation.

James' church lived in the midst of this collapsing world. Although the church as a whole was growing and spreading across the world, believers felt oppressed. In their suffering, their tendency was to imitate the world and try to gain power within the church. There was also a weariness about the church and an impatience with waiting for Christ's return. The struggle for power combined with this weariness to produce internal factions, gossip, and complaints. Since the church was economically insecure, church members tended to curry favor with the few wealthy members, to hold back on charitable giving, and generally to "look out for number one." James senses a general worldliness despite good attendance at services. This is the situation James addresses with a stinging letter designed to shake them out of their lethargy.

Thematic Emphases[4]

Even to begin to write about theological themes discovered in the Epistle of James takes a little boldness, for the German New Testament scholar Martin Dibelius denied just such a possibility in his commentary (1921).[5] James is ethical teaching, a miscellaneous collection from various sources without any internal coherence among its various themes. Fortunately, however, research on James has moved beyond the work of Dibelius, beginning with scholars in his native Germany. In other words, the study of James has now moved from the period of form-criticism, which studies works in pieces, into that of redaction-criticism, which studies them as edited wholes;[6] the age of the string-of-pearls conception of the letter is past, and its essential theological unity is ready for exploration. Furthermore, at least one author has found a literary form, that of the literary or secondary letter with a doubled introduction, into which the epistle as a whole fits.[7] It is this overall form that gives a basis for extracting the theological themes of the epistle.

If, then, it is legitimate to look at James as an edited unity, one will discover that the epistle is primarily a theology of suffering, an expression of a Jewish theology of suffering with a long history before James' Christian version. Naturally, it is impossible to give a full discussion of the development of this theological concept; it will suffice to simply sketch some of the major points, leaving the details for the commentary text.

Within the context of a theology of suffering, James' primary concern is with the health of the community. The concern of the work is not simply suffering, but suffering within the context of communal concern. This means that it is wrong to read the epistle with an individualistic focus; that would be to miss the chief concern of the author. Rather, the author addresses the behavior of individuals because that behavior has an impact upon the life of the community. One should note that all of the various sins and behaviors addressed have to do with the solidarity of the Christian community, not simply with the internal life of the faithful or the relationship of the faithful to the non-Christian world. As such, the ethic of James has some great similarities to the ethic of the Dead Sea Scrolls community.

The starting place for this theology is suffering. Thus James begins with a primary focus on trials. The concept itself has two sides. First, a trial is a test that in the context of James comes from the suffering of the Christian.[8] It is something to be endured, to teach patience, and to lead to perfect virtue. This is essentially the message of James 1:2–4. Second, a trial is a challenge to the faith of the believer. As with Israel in the wilderness, the temptation in the face of suffering is to lose faith and to challenge God.

One buckles in the test and blames God for the failure, for a sovereign God ought not to have sent such a test. Here one finds the focus of 1:12-15.

The call in the Epistle of James is for supernatural joy in the face of the testing situation. This joy because of belief in the coming of Christ and his reward is apparent in both halves of the doubled opening statement, 1:2 and 1:12. There is a blessedness in coming into the testing situation, for the test itself is a mark that one has chosen to be on the side of God, as R. Jonathan (an early rabbi cited in the Talmud and other Jewish literature) later said,

> A potter does not examine defective vessels. . . . What then does he examine? Only the sound vessels. . . . Similarly, the Holy One, blessed be he, tests not the wicked but the righteous, as it says, "The Lord trieth the righteous."[9]

The test can lead to reward (i.e., a "reward" or "a crown of life" [James 1:12], presumably from the hands of Christ, as in Rev. 2:10) on the Judgment Day. Thus there is every reason to rejoice in anticipation of the reward, if one stands firm.

Naturally, the problem in James is that some are not standing firm. To what can one attribute this failure to stand in the test? The reaction of the individual involved is to blame God, but James rules that out with his use of the phrase "God cannot be tempted by evil," which is better translated, "God ought not to be tested by evil people" (1:13), for this would be the same failure that Israel showed in the wilderness. Instead James points out, in continuity with the tendency of later Judaism, that God does not send the test (although James is not intending to make a statement about the sovereignty of God); rather, suffering becomes a test of faith to human beings because of the evil impulse within, that is, "evil desire" (1:14).

At this point James has combined two streams in the theology of later Judaism. The evil impulse, or evil *yêṣer* (the Hebrew name), was as well known in later Judaism as the problem of suffering. Human beings have within them an undifferentiated drive or desire that pushes them to good as well as evil. When it impels marriage, the building of a house, and the procreation of children, it is good. But since it is undifferentiated desire, it will just as forcefully impel one to adultery, theft, and murder. This appeal to the evil impulse not only allows James to put the blame for failure squarely on the shoulders of the individual (1:13–15), but it also allows him to point to the same force as the reason for the lack of harmony in the community (4:1–8). In the latter passage, one sees that the evil impulse is fundamentally tied to the world, so when one is motivated by this impulse one is bound to be tied to the world and thus put in a position of enmity with respect to God. Here one finds the person in a situation not unlike that of Paul in Romans 7: He has mentally accepted the proper theology and the need to serve God but is so tied to this life that suffering brings compromise and the breakdown of Christian virtue.

Yet in pointing to the evil impulse and thus to the individual, James does not in any way wish to negate the dualistic eschatological context within which he is working. One notes first of all that when he thinks of Christ he does not do so with reference to a theology of the cross as Paul might but rather with reference to him as the exalted Lord in heaven who is soon to return. Thus the three ways in which he thinks of him are (1) Lord (six times), (2) judge (5:9), and (3) king (if "royal law" in 2:8 refers to Jesus). The focus is on the return of the exalted Christ, which is "near," even "at the door" (5:7–11). It is in light of the coming of this person in apocalyptic judgment (when God breaks into history in the end of the world) that one ought to endure, for as in the case of Job, patient endurance will be rewarded, and that reasonably soon. James presents a simple teaching about Christ more resembling that found in the early speeches in Acts than to the more complex ideas of Paul. He also has a strongly apocalyptic eschatology (a teaching about God's relationship to the world focused on his judgment in the end of the world) like that found in Mark 13 or Revelation.

Second, one notes that James sees another side to the problem of suffering than that of the evil impulse. In rabbinic Judaism and in the Dead Sea Scrolls, it was not unusual to speak in one breath of evil impulse or spirit within the individual and in the next, of Satan without, who leads the individual astray. James fits into the same camp of limited dualism as these (or, for that matter, the synoptic Gospels, i.e., the first three Gospels). In James 3:13–18 the cause of community strife is traced to a "wisdom" (James himself only defines it negatively, "not-the-wisdom-from-heaven," but surely the teachers dividing the community thought of it as wisdom) that is described as earthly, natural (i.e., devoid of the Spirit), and demonic. Particularly this latter term leads one to suspect that the author would, if pressed, trace the origin of sin to something other than the evil impulse within the individual. In 4:7 he makes this fact clear, for in addressing those who in the test are giving in, who are driven by pleasure or desire, he cries out, "Submit yourselves, then, to God. Resist the devil, and he will flee from you!" Thus for James there is a tempter without as well as a tempter within. The testing situation is not from God but from the evil one. Yet the failure in the situation cannot be blamed upon the devil, for it is the evil impulse within that leads one to fail under the stress of the test.

Having observed the problem of suffering in the community, however, one should further note that there is a specific theological context for the suffering, which is the piety of the poor. It had become clear by the time of the postexilic Jewish community that piety was not always rewarded with wealth and success. Under the persecution of the King of the Seleucid Empire in Antioch, Antiochus Epiphanes (170–164 B.C.), and the Jewish Hasmonean rulers (priest-kings descended from the priest Matthias, ruling 167–63 B.C.), it appeared far more certain that piety would be rewarded with poverty and suffering in this world. Yet God in the Old Testament is said to be the deliverer of the poor and oppressed. This fact is true and was felt to be true to such a degree that people would call upon God, pressing their claim on the basis that they were in fact poor and oppressed (e.g., Ps. 86:1). Thus in later Judaism many of the pious groups came to see that their poverty was in fact a sign of their election by God—they were the community of the poor. In some few cases the opposite conclusion was also drawn: The rich were bound for perdition (1 Enoch 94–105, 108).

This theology is found in the New Testament, as well as in Judaism, notably in the Sermon on the Mount, particularly in the Lucan version (Luke 6). It is here that the sayings tradition (sometimes called Q[10]) preserves sayings of Jesus that bless the poor (the "poor in spirit" of Matthew not intending to mean less than literal poverty) and, in Luke, curse the rich. Throughout the

Gospels there are numerous references to the poor and to the danger of wealth that must be understood in light of this tradition. James draws heavily upon this teaching.

For James the elect community is the poor. God has "chosen those who are poor in the eyes of the world to be rich in faith and to inherit the kingdom" (2:5). Earlier he has said, "The brother in humble circumstances ought to take pride in his high position" (1:9). Furthermore, it is clear that the community contains many who are not all wealthy, that the relatively wealthy members are unusual and thus potentially powerful, and that at least a portion of the community works as day laborers. These data fit with what is known elsewhere of the early church in general and the Palestinian church in particular.

By way of contrast, James has little use for the rich. The very term *rich* denotes one who is outside of the community and on the way to judgment. Thus the wealthy in 1:10–11 are said to wither and perish like grass. In 5:1–6 James roundly curses the wealthy as being the oppressors of the poor and earning the judgment of God that is about to fall upon them. In 2:6–7 the rich are accused of using the courts to oppress the poor and of blaspheming the name of Christ. In places where it is arguable that relatively wealthy Christians may be in view, James uses a circumlocution rather than the term *rich* and then has little but criticism for these persons (2:1–4, 4:13–17).

Given these data about the piety of the poor, then, one can see the dimensions of James' concern a little more clearly. First, the church, like the Dead Sea Scrolls community, is primarily the community of the poor. This would be true both literally and in terms of its own self-concept. The church does suffer from its relative impoverishment. Second, the financially poor condition of the church is in part the result of perceived persecution by the rich. It is clear that James' community is not suffering the type of legal persecution leading to martyrdom later found in the Roman Empire, but it does appear to be suffering some forms of discrimination from a group it conceives of as "the rich." Some of this suffering may have been just because Christians were poor. After all, as is shown by the revolt of the Jews in A.D. 70 (as well as by several disturbances among the poor in Rome), there was a great deal of general feeling among the poor against the rich.

But if Christians were a relatively despised minority, one would expect them to feel more of the brunt of the oppression (the wealthy could count on the courts being less favorable to such a group) and to attribute this persecution to religious motives.

The situation puts the church into a context in which it has become attractive to form some type of compromise with the world, as James will put it, breaking the solidarity of the community. First, one sees the church giving in, in that it panders to the wealthy. This, claims James, is fundamental disloyalty to the law of Christ. Second, there is a tendency to avoid the demands of charity; but James reminds them that this is to reveal an essentially defective faith and to fail in the test, unlike Abraham. Third, there is the temptation to seek wealth oneself; this forms the basis of James' warning to the merchant group (better: peddler group) in the church (4:13–17).

A second reaction to the outward pressure may or may not have been directly connected to the situation, but James at least connects it to the same underlying cause. The community under pressure tends to split into bickering factions, each one trying to get control, push its own teaching, and take advantage of its own position. This appears to be the problem addressed in chapters 3 and 4. Needless to say, such reactions to stress are not in the least unknown in other ages.

Given a community including the poor undergoing testing and finding within themselves weakness rather than the patient endurance of the prophets (i.e., they were not willing to wait and allow the Lord on his return to set affairs right), one immediately asks about the role of faith and grace in this situation. It is here that James' epistle has proved most difficult, particularly because his thought has not often been seen within its larger context.

First, James apparently has two definitions of faith. One is found chiefly in chapter 1 and 5 (1:3, 6; 2:1, 5; 5:15) and could be roughly translated as "commitment" or "trust." Its opposite is "hypocrisy" or "double-minded" (1:8; 4:8), a divided mind in which the evil impulse is dominant and thus a mind that does not look solely to God for help but also to the world. Here faith is characteristic of one who is enduring the test; it is a definition reasonably close to the Pauline definition of faith. The other definition of faith is found only in 2:14-26. In this passage faith is simply "intellectual belief" (so 1:19); it certainly does not have the element of commitment and trust, that is, the personal character, so evident in the Pauline and the Johannine conceptions.

Second, for James, true commitment will result in obedience. This is clear whether one looks at 2:8ff., where the law as interpreted through Christ is taken for granted as the standard of Christian behavior, much as it is in Matthew. Whether one looks at 1:19-27, where the reception of the word results in doing the word, or whether one looks at 2:14-26, where the true believer has faith and works, true commitment results in obedience. Thus faith is in fact a resource in the situation if it is the first type of faith, a commitment to God that will disregard the world, for such trust will allow one to act upon the word, the law, and obey it in deeds of righteousness. The other type of faith is useless.

Third, James shows no direct contact with Paul's thought. It is precisely in the passage of 2:14-26 that this fact is most evident. His definitions of each of the three critical terms, "faith," "actions," and "considered righteous," as well as his use of the Abraham example (which itself was already embedded in Christian ethical teaching and not an exclusive possession of Paul), differ from Paul. If James is reacting to Paul at all, it is to a Paul so distorted and misunderstood that it can hardly be said to be Paul.

Faith, then, in its first meaning of "trust," is a commitment to God. This commitment yields far more than simply the words of the law, even those words as interpreted by Christ. Commitment leads to prayer, and prayer produces the wisdom of God. Here it is important to note two facts about wisdom. On the one hand, it is that which is needed in the situation of testing (1:5), for it brings one to moral perfection. On the other hand, it is a gift from above (3:13ff. and probably 1:17 as well) that grants a series of community-preserving virtues when it motivates one. What, then, is the meaning of this gift from God? It is clear that it is not the typical Jewish identification—wisdom is Torah, or law—for the law is certainly separate from wisdom in James. Nor would it be proper to speak of a "wisdom Christology," for there is no evidence that Christ is spoken of as wisdom in this book. But it is quite clear that the function of wisdom in James is parallel to that of the Spirit in much of the rest of the New Testament. Thus one has in James an extension of the identification of the Spirit with wisdom. This was previously known in Judaism and in some places included the expectation that wisdom would be God's gift to the elect in the new age. In James, wisdom is indeed God's gift to the elect. It is a power within the individual that produces the needed virtues for community life (3:13–18, the vice and virtue catalog being similar to the function of Spirit in Gal. 5 and the Dead Sea Scroll 1 QS 4) and enables one to withstand the test. In doing this it counteracts the evil desire that may be the "wisdom from below," and thus it functions similarly to the spirit in Romans 8 or the good impulse in later rabbinic thought.

Wisdom, then, fits into a context of prayer. Prayer in 1:5–8 is certainly the request for wisdom, much as in Luke 10:21–24 and 11:9–13 prayer is a request for the Spirit. In James 4:1–3 the complaint is not that the people are not praying but that the prayer is wrongly directed; their focus is on the world and their worldly needs—they are not asking for the proper item, that is, divine wisdom. Their motives in asking are already controlled by the evil impulse. In the final context, 5:13–18, prayer functions similarly to confession in 1 John and yields the healing attributed to the Spirit in 1 Corinthians 12. The connection in this case may well be that the community is the real possessor of divine wisdom, and thus the elders (perhaps the truly wise teachers of chapter 3) will be those full of that divine power. At the least it is the same type of prayer (prayer of faith, i.e., trust) that raises the sick and calls down wisdom. It may well be that for James the divine wisdom itself (i.e., the Spirit) is a possession of the community as much as of the individual.

This hardly does more than simply sketch out the theology of James with the briefest of descriptions. Much more could be and has been written. But this brief sketch shows us an author concerned with a community undergoing suffering. He sees his community as the elect poor being tested by the devil. Outside the community, they face the oppression of the rich; within the group, they face dissension; and within each, they must face the evil impulse. They must and can stand and even rejoice in this, but to do so they must trust unreservedly in God, refuse to hope in the world and its security at all, act on the word that they have heard, persevere in their identity as the poor by acting charitably, and above all, seek the divine wisdom that enables them to live up to the total demand of God. In so doing they will endure until the Lord who is at the door indeed arrives.

James and Jesus

It is clear to any casual reader of James that his writing is very close to the teaching of Jesus. In particular James is very close to the teaching of Jesus recorded in the Sermon on the Mount (Matt. 5-7) or the Sermon on the Plain (Luke 6). This fact is underlined in that in all late Jewish and Christian literature, with one exception (1 Enoch), only James and Jesus pronounce woes on the rich.

The problem this raises is that James never directly cites a word of Jesus; he never says "Jesus said" or "the Lord said." Would not the Lord's brother refer to him directly? Would not a person so saturated with Jesus' ideas quote him at least once? The answer is that James does quote Jesus at least once, but even there he does not name his source (5:12). This leaves the reader with the probability that other verses in James (e.g., 3:18; 4:18) are sayings of Jesus that were not recorded in the Gospels.

Behind this phenomenon lies a feature of the early church. Before the Gospels were produced, there were probably some written records of Jesus' teaching (Luke refers to some sources in Luke 1:1-4), but the basic tradition was oral. Since Jesus was Lord and Head of the church, his teaching was its foundation and rule of life. Early Christians memorized this teaching much as Jews memorized that of their teachers. Further evidence of this lies in the Gospel of Matthew, where the teaching of Jesus is divided into five blocks (chapters 5-7, 10, 13, 18, 24-25), each of which has a single theme. These are designed for easy memory (since most Christians could neither read nor afford books), with numerical sequences and link-words being used to aid memory. Later, after the Gospels appeared, their teaching was compressed into handbooks like the Didache for teaching to new converts.

The result of this process was that most people in the church had learned much of the teaching of Jesus by heart. The letter of James is designed to take advantage of this fact. Where he quotes Jesus directly without saying so, he realizes Christians will know who originally made the statement. It is even quite possible that most of the proverbs and short sayings in James came from Jesus. But more important are his allusions to Jesus, some thirty-five times in the epistle, or once every three verses (e.g., 2:5 and Matt. 5:3, 5; 11:5, 2:6 and Luke 18:3; 2:8 and Matt. 22:39–40). The early Christian reader would immediately recognize that James was reminding them of sayings of Jesus. They, along with the Old Testament, are James' authority. In the Old Testament he basically calls on stories; with Jesus he calls on teaching. The combination means that James' message could only be resisted by rejecting Jesus as well.

James, then, is a handbook of an early Christian community. It shows how the leader of the community drew on the foundation teaching of the community to address contemporary issues. Thus James serves as a model for the church as to how to use the teaching of Jesus. For him the teachings of Jesus are not merely interesting insights irrelevant to modern life or applicable only in the millennium. For him, Jesus is Lord and his teaching is the rule of life. Discipleship is not an optional extra but what it means to be a Christian. What remains is to apply the teaching to specific situations and to draw appropriate conclusions, that is, to preach using the teaching of Jesus as a text, expressed or unexpressed. James is a model of how this was done in the first decades of the church, an authoritative example for the modern church to heed and emulate.

Notes

1. F. F. Bruce, *New Testament History* (New York: Doubleday, 1972), p. 370.

2. F. O. Francis, "The Form and Function of the Opening and Closing Paragraphs of James and 1 John," *ZNW* 61 (1970), pp. 110–26.

3. Ibid.

4. This section is an edited version of "Theological Perspectives on the Epistle of James," *Journal of the Evangelical Theological Society* 23 (1980), pp. 93–104, reproduced here by permission of the editor.

5. M. Dibelius, *James*.

6. Form criticism, which more or less began with Martin Dibelius, focused on breaking the text into the units in which it was orally transmitted (e.g., proverbs, sayings, stories, sermons). Redaction criticism, which began in the 1950s, focuses on how the final editor of the work put the traditions be used together into a unified whole with a single theology. Both were initially developed for the Gospels, where the evangelists worked with sayings of Jesus, and only later were applied to the epistles.

7. F. O. Francis, "The Opening and Closing Paragraphs of James and 1 John."

8. Suffering in the New Testament is something which one endures because one is a Christian. In both Greek vocabulary use and attitudes toward suffering the New Testament differentiates it from sickness, which all people experience, Christian or not. James shows this difference clearly in 5:7–18. In 5:7–11 suffering is to be endured; in 5:14–18 sickness is to be prayed for and healed. See further P. H. Davids, "Suffering and Illness in the New Testament," in *Understanding Power Evangelism* (forthcoming; title tentative), eds. Douglas Pennoyer and C. Peter Wagner (Ventura, Calif.: Regal Books, 1989).

9. Genesis Rabba 55:2.

10. Q is a symbol used by New Testament scholars for those traditions Matthew and Luke have in common but that are not found in Mark. Some believe Q was a written document, others that it was an oral tradition.

§1 Wisdom for Life's Tests (James 1:1–27)

1:1 / The letter from James opens with a simple and direct greeting. The writer identifies himself simply as **James, a servant of God**. There was only one James so well known in the early church that he would need no other form of identification, and that was James the Just, brother of Jesus, leader of the church in Jerusalem. The readers are expected to recognize the name.

Yet for all his prominence and important position in the church (so important that the letter from Jude begins, "Jude, a servant of Jesus Christ and a brother of James"), the title used is very modest. He is simply **a servant**. It is possible that he is thinking of himself as someone like Moses, chosen of God and taken into his service (Deut. 34:5; Josh. 1:2, Num. 12:7), but more likely it simply reflects the humility of the author. The most exalted statement he can make about himself is not his leadership of the church or his relationship to Jesus, but the fact that he, like every other Christian, is a slave of God and of Jesus. He calls Jesus **The Lord Jesus Christ**, for he is thinking of him as his heavenly, exalted Lord, who is about to return in glory to set things right in the world. It is this picture of Jesus that dominates the letter throughout.

James sends his greetings to **the twelve tribes scattered among the nations**. On the one hand, he sees the church as a united body or a distinct nation in the world. Believers are God's people as the Romans are Caesar's people and Egyptians are Pharaoh's. They are his chosen ones here on earth. Yet they are not a powerful group, for they are **scattered**. They are not a physically united group; they do not have a land they may call their own. Instead they are spread throughout the nations, belonging, yet never being one of the people among whom they live, living out their lives as foreigners in the land in which they were born.

Their dignity is not in strength or numbers but in the fact that they belong to God.

James begins the letter itself by introducing his three main topics—trials, wisdom, and wealth: (1) A proper perspective gives one joy despite a difficult situation, although in order to stand in such a situation one will need divine wisdom. (2) The person who prays for this wisdom needs to pray from a committed position. Without commitment one will receive nothing. (3) One of the chief trials of life and tests of commitment is wealth and how one uses it. There is no need to fear the rich—their end is at hand.

1:2 / James addresses his readers as **brothers**, which means that he considers them members of the church in good standing. There is a warmth in his address that continues throughout the letter despite his criticism of them. He is one with his readers and shares their weaknesses, as he will show more graphically in 3:1–2.

The readers are to **consider it pure joy** when they suffer **trials of many kinds**. The trials to which James refers are the testing and refining situations in life, hard situations in which faith is sorely tried, such as persecution, a difficult moral choice, or a tragic experience. James does not gloss over the reality of the suffering involved—the tears, the pain, the sweat. Instead he points to a transformed perspective of those trials. If one looks at the difficult situation not merely from the perspective of the immediate problem but also from the perspective of the end result God is producing, one can have a deep joy. This is not a surface happiness, but an anticipation of future reward in the end-times (eschatological joy). It is not only possible, but necessary (thus James commands it), for without it one may become so bogged down in present problems as to abandon the faith and give up the struggle altogether. Only with God's perspective, thus considering oneself already fortunate in anticipation of God's future reward, can the faith be maintained against the pressures of life.

1:3 / One reason it is possible to believe oneself to be fortunate in adversity is that the suffering produces a good result even now. With Joseph one might say, "You meant evil against me; but God meant it for good" (Gen. 50:20). The process of testing faith is like the tempering of steel: the heat, rather than destroying the steel, makes it stronger. The apocryphal book Sirach (2:5) uses another image: "For gold is proved in the fire, and men acceptable to God in the furnace of affliction." The process is difficult, but the result is good.

James assumes the good result when he writes, **the testing of your faith develops perseverance**. The test has to do with the fact that they have faith, that there is "pure gold" in them. They should not look fearfully at testing, but look through it, for the result will be **perseverance**. This ability is hardly a virtue to be winked at. First, it is a virtue that only suffering and trials will produce. Second, it yields to a stable character, a firm, settled disposition of faith: It is a heroic virtue. A person possessing such a virtue could be trusted to hold out, whatever the circumstances. Such people were surely in demand as leaders in the church. Third, it relates the believer to other believers who were noted in Jewish tradition for this virtue: Abraham, who was put through the fire ten times (Jubilees 17:18; 19:8), Joseph, who went from trial to trial before becoming ruler over Egypt (Testament of Joseph 2:7; 10:1), or Job, who endured patiently a series of almost unbelievable sufferings, only to be rewarded in the end (James 5:11; Testament of Job).

There is no question that this virtue is important, just as there is no question that the means of getting it are unpopular. But the Christian is called to face into the fact: However difficult and unpleasant the test may seem, God is perfecting the Christian's character through it.

1:4 / **Perseverance**, however, is not a passive, teeth-gritting virtue, but a development in which the character is firmed up and shaped around the central commitment to Christ. It does not happen overnight, for it is a process. The process needs to **finish its work**, or "have its complete effect," for it is the shaping of the whole person that is at issue. One must be careful not to short-circuit it: to pull the metal out of the fire too soon, to abort the developing child, to resist the schooling—to use three metaphors often used to describe the process. James does not see a

single end to the process, such as the development of love as a
super-virtue (Rom. 13:8; 2 Pet. 1:6) or the fruit of the Spirit (Gal.
5:6; Rom. 6:22)—although he would have certainly approved of
such—for the goal is far more global. The person is formed, not
just partly or simply morally, but totally, as a whole being, and
is thus to be **mature and complete, not lacking anything**.

In speaking of the person as perfect James is not thinking
of sinless perfection but is probably referring to a concept like
that found in Matthew 5:48, "Be perfect, therefore, as your heavenly Father is perfect." The concept is that of a commitment to
the command of God in all its depth and radicality, a commitment that calls anything less than total obedience sin and repents
and seeks forgiveness, a commitment that, rather than reducing
the word to the cultural "pagan" standard of the world, seeks to
be shaped and formed by it. In other words, James is referring
to mature Christian character: It is **mature** in that it is well developed; it is **complete** in that every virtue and insight is in place;
it is **not lacking anything**, but mirrors Christ. This is what adversity should produce in the Christian if he or she will allow
it. But it is not a passive process; the believer has to permit this
to happen. There is an imperative involved (a better translation
might be "allow perseverance to finish its work"). It is possible
to short-circuit the process and thus not to develop properly and
to live through the suffering in vain.

1:5 / James now turns to his second theme and what appears to be a totally new topic, that of wisdom and prayer. It is
indeed a major theme of the letter, but it is not unrelated to what
goes before. If person hears a call to be perfect, he or she would
certainly cry, "Help! Who can do it?" (like Paul's "Who is sufficient for these things?" 2 Cor. 2:16; 3:5–6). Divine help is necessary, and divine help in James comes in the form of wisdom
(cf. 3:13 ff.). Christians should indeed lack nothing, but in order
to do this they need divine wisdom.

James shares this recognition. **If any of you lacks wisdom,
he should ask God**. He can do this with full confidence that God
gives generously to all. Here James draws on the Jesus tradition
(the yet unwritten sayings of Jesus that later formed the Gospels),
for Jesus promised God would give his children what they ask

(Matt. 7:7–11; Mark 11:24; Luke 11:9–13; John 15:7). What better gift could they request than the wisdom needed to withstand the trials they face. God **gives** it, for God is a good giver; God gives **generously**, which means that he gives without mental reservations, that he gives simply, with a single heart. He is not looking for some hidden return from believers; he does not have mixed motives or grudging feelings. In fact, he gives not just generously but **without finding fault**. That is, he does not complain about the gift or its cost. He is not a "fool," who "has many eyes instead of one. He gives little and upbraids much, he opens his mouth like a herald; today he lends and tomorrow he asks back" (Sirach 20:14–15). No, God gives true gifts: no complaining, no criticizing (What? You need help *again*?), no mixed motives, no reluctance. Free, generous, even spendthrift giving characterizes the Christian's God.

And what a gift he gives! He gives wisdom, which in this letter is the equivalent of the Holy Spirit, a gift that James' readers, as former Jews, would recognize (as the people of the Dead Sea Scrolls did) as one of the gifts of the age to come. Wisdom comes to the Christian through Christ (1 Cor. 1:24; 2:4–6). This surely is what is needed to withstand trials and come to perfection.

1:6 / Not everyone, however, receives that wisdom requested. "Where is that spiritual power?" one might ask. "If God is so generous, where is the wisdom I need to discern the situation, to withstand the test, and to come to perfection?" Such questions were certainly asked, for James provides an answer: **But when he asks, he must believe and not doubt.**

First, **he must believe**, that is, one must ask in the context of faith. Faith here is not simply intellectual knowledge (as it will be in 2:19). James has no thought that one simply has to give intellectual assent to a doctrine to receive the blessing (e.g., God will give what Christians ask; therefore he will give them wisdom if they ask for it). James does not appear to be calling for research into the truth of a matter (e.g., that the promise really is one given by Jesus or that out of a hundred people who prayed all received their request, while only fifty of a similar group who did not pray had a satisfactory outcome), but for commitment. Therefore he is also not speaking of faith as an emotional feeling (i.e., if only people could keep feeling that God is really giving wisdom to them will they receive it). Certainly, this is how James has been interpreted by later commentators both in modern popular religion and in ancient times. But James is not trying to encourage believers to stuff their doubts deep within and to drum up an emotional *feeling* of certainty, but to commit themselves. Faith for James is a single-minded commitment to God that trusts in God because God is God. Thus faith remains resting in God despite doubt and holds on through testing. Faith is the "but if not" of Daniel's friends (Dan. 3:18); the "though he slay me yet will I trust him" of Job (Job 13:15). It is a confident trust in God or a resting in God despite the outward circumstances.

Because of this fact, the opposite of faith (**not doubt**) is doubt. The person who doubts is not doubting that God will do something *specific*, but is doubting in general. "Does God really act *today*?" or more deeply expressed, "Can I trust God to do the best for me or must I look out for myself?" Here James may be applying a tradition from Jesus like that in Matthew 21:21: "I tell you the truth, if you have faith and do not doubt, . . . you can do what was done to this fig tree."

The doubter is **like a wave of the sea**. The picture is graphic. The doubter is "one who lives in inner conflict between trust and distrust of God." (F. Mussner, *Der Jakobusbrief* [Freiburg: Herder, 1967], p. 70.) In a service of worship this person is caught up in the music, the words of praise, or the exhortation of the sermon and trusts God completely. Outside, the same person faces the winds of adversity and, instead of trusting *despite feelings,* gives in and believes that only his or her own resources and cleverness can help. Like wind-tossed water, an unstable Christian sways back and forth.

1:7–8 / That man, says James (to clearly distinguish this individual from other people with a stable faith), **should not think he will receive anything from the Lord**. Obviously James cannot be sure that such a person, or even a wicked blasphemer, for that matter, will receive nothing from God. God is gracious and kind, often giving more than he has promised and always giving far more than people deserve. Sun and rain come to the good and the evil alike. But such a person wavering between God and the

world ought not to *expect* to receive something from God. Such
a person has no right to expect **anything**, much less wisdom, for
he or she is not following the proper principles. The promises
of the gospel all assume a commitment of the individual to, and
trust in, God (e.g., the "in my name" formula, John 14:14). Without this trust there is a more basic issue to be settled than that
of the item asked for: The more basic issue is that of trust. Until
one has dealt with this issue, one is in no position to begin
praying.

This person, claims James, **is a double-minded man, unstable in all he does**. The pre-Christian Jew Sirach had already
said, "My son, disobey not the fear of the Lord, and approach
it not with a double heart" (1:28), and, "Woe unto the fearful
hearts and faint hands, and unto the sinner that goes two ways
. . . woe unto you who have lost your endurance" (2:12-14). James
has the same concern for this person of a double mind. If a
person's mind is split and he or she really does not know whom
to trust, one can hardly have confidence in such a person. Such
a one is not just undecided but, in fact, **unstable**. Now, indeed,
he or she may "trust" in God and be part of the church, but with
a heart filled with doubt, this person is emotionally keeping op-
tions open and other lines of support clear. There is a basic instability within that will eventually become evident in behavior.
You cannot trust such a person, for he or she is like Aesop's crow,
trying to walk down two paths at once. The implied call is for
commitment. "Put all your eggs in one basket," and make that
basket God. Without commitment, prayer is in vain. James 4:1-10
will make this crystal clear.

1:9 / One sign of trust in God is the ability to see beyond present circumstances. Here James returns to a theme of
verse 2 and makes it more concrete when he says, **The brother
in humble circumstances ought to take pride**. . . . The person
must be **the brother**, for only the Christian has the resources to
see beyond the present circumstances. The believer is a member
of the community that belongs to the coming age but also a member of a community of the poor in the present age. The term
humble circumstances indicates not just someone who lacks material goods and thus leads a hand-to-mouth existence struggling

to get the bare necessities of life (and perhaps at times not succeeding), but also someone socially despised. This believer is a person whose lot in life has humbled him or her.

This believer is to **take pride in his high position**. The call is for Christians to exult or take pride in their state. What a contrast to their perceived social standing! What could such people possibly take pride in? The answer is "in their exalted position." It is not that God will lift Christians up in the future but that God has already lifted them up. Here you have the poor Christian, who knows he or she is an heir to the universe (Matt. 5:3, 5; James 2:5). This is the rejoicing of Mary, who saw God filling the hungry and exalting the poor in her own person (Luke 1:52–53). This person realizes that the outward, depressed circumstances are not the essence of the situation. Such a Christian is not merely a rich person, not simply one of the powerful of Palestine, but a child of God destined as heir to a worldwide kingdom. He or she does have plenty in which to take pride, but it is only apparent to those with faith and trust.

1:10 / The **rich**, however, are hardly in such a position. They surely seem in a position in which to take pride. After all they suffer no lack of material goods, famine does not haunt them, their children are well fed and healthy, they are powerful in the city, and they receive respect from all around them (cf. Ps. 73). Should they not rejoice in their prosperity as a gift from God? Not so, writes James, they **should** instead **take pride in** their **low position**.

Two comments may clarify this reasoning. First, **the one who is rich** may mislead the reader into supplying "Christian," which does not appear in the Greek text. "Rich" in James always indicates one outside the community, a nonbelieving person. The rich, in fact, are the oppressors of the community (2:6; 5:1–6)

Second, the call to **take pride** is ironic in two senses. On the one hand, when the rich are converted they share their goods with and identify with the poor "scum" they formerly despised and persecuted. They become one of the group that calls itself the poor and that is exalted by God and despised by society. This is something, indeed, to take pride in, but it is precisely in losing their status as rich and being "brought down" to the humble level of the church that the rich have anything in which to take pride. On the other hand, since James expects most of the rich not to repent but to fall under God's judgment, there is irony in calling them to take pride, because what they are at present proud about is indeed their humiliation. It is, as 5:1–6 will make clear, the very evidence that will condemn them, that will, as it were, eat their flesh in the Day of Judgment. They are children rejoicing in their mischief, but a parent is about to turn the corner, and the very object of their joy, the evidence of their disobedience, will humiliate them within seconds. They are rich—rich fools (Luke 12:13–21).

The fact is the rich **will pass away like a wild flower.** Wealth is very impressive, and the rich seem very important now, but if one looks at them from God's perspective, one sees that the impressiveness is that of a soap bubble. Death is coming and the wealth will disappear and the rich will descend stripped naked to the depths of Hades (as shown by Job 15:30 and Prov. 2:8, in the Old Testament; in the Apocrypha, Sirach 14:11–19; 2 Baruch 82:3–9; or in the New Testament, Matt. 6:19–21.) Again the proper perspective is critical. Only with God's perspective, the perspective of the coming age, can one recognize this truth and the bitter irony it contains.

1:11 / The picture James uses to impress this idea on his readers is a phenomenon most dramatically observed in Palestine. The anemones and cyclamen bloom beautifully in the morning, but as the sun rises and the day becomes hotter they droop, wither, and die. By evening the once impressive blooms are gone, never to be again. The picture is drawn, perhaps, from Isaiah 40:6–8 (also used in 1 Pet. 1:24), but the meaning is uniquely James'. The wealthy person is the flower that looks so impressive. But from the perspective of heaven this person's situation is precarious indeed. Soon some trouble or disease will come, and where will that rich person be then? In the face of death wealth is absolutely meaningless (cf. Job 15:30; Prov. 2:8; Ps. 73; Matt. 6:19–21). The wealthy will **fade away** as they go **about [their] business.** Theirs will not be an eternal remembrance with glory as they hoped, but they will go down to the dust like any mortal, and slowly their monuments and very memory will crumble and disappear into oblivion. And that was all the rich had, for unlike the poor, who were "lifted up" and thus had an eternal place with God, the rich had all their lot here on earth and thus descend forever into darkness and oblivion from the very midst of their **business**.

At this point James begins the second half of his opening statement. Although he discusses the same topics, he does not repeat himself, for each topic is advanced. The inward causes of defection in the test are discussed rather than the benefits of trials in general. God's good gift in relationship to the problem of speech, rather than in relationship to prayer and wisdom, is discussed. Putting faith into practice (which means sharing generously) is his focus now, rather than a discussion of the true standing of rich and poor. All of these topics will eventually coalesce in his major discussions and in his conclusion.

1:12 / James begins with a beatitude: **Blessed is the man**. Like Jesus in Matthew 5:3–12, he pronounces a surprising group blessed, those **who persevere under trial**. It is not just the person who is tested who is considered happy or blessed but the person who endures or remains faithful. In 1:2–4 James has said that testing produces endurance; now he states that enduring creates true blessedness. Yet James is neither a masochist nor a stoic, neither claims that trials are fun nor that one should enjoy pain. Rather, he points out that the trials serve a purpose, the experiential proof of the reality of faith, and that that should give one the perspective for deep joy. From reactions to testing one knows one is truly committed and that **when** [one] **has stood the test** a reward will come. A person passing a test is like silver being assayed and receiving the hallmark of purity: God marks the person "approved"; his or her faith is sound.

Such a person will receive a *reward*, that is (in the Greek idiom), "a crown of life." This pictures the last judgment as if it were a judges' stand at the end of a race (cf. 2 Tim. 4:8). The victorious runner approaches and a laurel wreath is set on his or her head. But this wreath is life itself (cf. Rev. 2:10), and not just one winner but all who finish the race (endure) receive the reward, for God has promised it to all **those who love him**. Salvation has only one price, an enduring love of God. With this prospect in mind, Christians can consider themselves truly blessed or fortunate despite outward circumstances, for they already taste the reward.

1:13 / There is, however, another possible response to a test: one can collapse and fail. Naturally someone about to "give in" does not want to take responsibility for the failure, for that would be totally inconsistent with a self-image of being a "good Christian," so he or she rationalizes: "The test was too hard; God is at fault for sending it."

James warns against such a reaction: **When tempted, no one should say, "God is tempting me."** Such a conclusion would readily suggest itself to James' monotheistic audience. Is God not sovereign? James refuses to answer this question, for such a discussion would obscure the real point. This person does not want deeper understanding, but an excuse. The claim that the test comes from God is not at heart a theological analysis but a placement of blame for the failure; it is an accusation.

James rejects this accusation for two reasons. First, "evil people should not put God to the test" (the phrase **God cannot be tempted by evil** is a misunderstanding of the Greek). Israel had done this many times (at least ten times: Num. 14:22); every time they faced suffering, they blamed God, doubting his will and ability to help them. But the Old Testament responded, "You shall not put the Lord your God to the test as you tested him at Massah" (Deut. 6:16). These Christians must not make the same mistakes Israel did, testing God.

Second, **he does** not **tempt anyone.** God does not wish evil on others; he does not cause evil; he does not test in the sense that he tries to trip someone up. James does not continue this explanation and clear up the issue of theodicy, for he has said enough for his purposes: God can be trusted. The cause of one's failure does not lie in God.

1:14 / One would expect James to continue by blaming the devil, but he does nothing of the kind, although he does believe that the devil plays a role (see James 4:7). Instead he writes, **Each one is tempted when, by his own evil desire, he is dragged away and enticed**. The real essence of temptation is not external,

that is, "the devil made me do it," but internal. "I have sinned
. . . by my fault, my very own fault," is the only "excuse." Whatever evil forces may set up the external circumstances, it is the
internal response that turns them into a test.

James clearly agrees with Paul. Using pictures from trap-
ping and fishing (**enticed** and **dragged away**) to show the allur-
ing nature of the "bait," its apparent harmlessness, and its
disastrous results, he reveals the enticer within, **evil desire**. Paul's
term for this entity is "sin," or "flesh," that is, fallen human nature: "I am a mortal man, sold as a slave to sin." "By myself I
can serve God's law only with my mind, while my human nature serves the law of sin" (Rom. 7:14, 25). The desires of people
are good by creation, for they lead them to enjoy creation, to eat,
to procreate, and so on, but they have been corrupted so that they
also lead them to lust, to steal, and to fornicate. The external situation could not affect people at all unless the internal voice of
their own nature was saying, "Go ahead; you deserve it; it feels
good."

1:15 / The desire of the person who gives in to the en-
ticement is here pictured as a prostitute or adulteress rather than
a trap or hook. She has successfully used her wiles, been ferti-
lized, and now carries within her a conceptus. Yet, "No one need
know," she whispers to her illegitimate lover. The inner defection
from the life of faith and trust need never be seen by others. But
the womb of the heart cannot hold the illegitimate thing forever;
desire's child comes to birth, and its name is **sin**. James has seen
a truth that Jesus proclaimed in Mark 7:20–23, "For from within,
out of men's hearts, come evil thoughts, . . . envy, slander, ar-
rogance and folly."

The test-desire-sin chain does not end there; it continues
one more link to **death**. Paul knew this truth (Rom. 6:23) as did
John (1 John 2:16–17; 3:14), but James puts it more graphically.
The child sin does not go away; instead this bastard offspring
grows to full maturity and then she too produces an offspring,
a monstrous, pathogenic, unwanted offspring—death. Here is the
result of failing the test. The person is on the way from desire
to sin, to maturity in sin, to death. Paul's chain in Romans 7:7–12
is reproduced here. James allows no inner deception. It must end

in death. There is only one escape, and that he gives in a contrasting chain in the following verses (1:16–18).

1:16 / **Don't be deceived, my dear brothers.** Deceived about what? Does this verse end the previous paragraph and refer to a belief that one could blame God or harbor desire or sin without any consequences? Or does it refer to a deception about where testing comes from (1:13)? Or does it head the following paragraph and refer to a failure to realize that God gives good and brings salvation? Structurally, the third option is preferred, for the address **my dear brothers** normally introduces a new paragraph. But this functions as a hinge verse: To be deceived about one of these items is to be deceived about them all, for the following paragraph is simply the negation of the previous one. If one blames God for a test, one is already edging toward sin and denying God's goodness. James believes his readers are true Christians (**brothers**) but he fears they might wander from faith, which is the implication of **don't be deceived**; he fears they might fall into the error of doubting God's goodness, which would be fatal to faith.

1:17 / In contrast to a view of God as sending a test stands the view that God gives good things: **Every good and perfect gift is from above.** The phrase itself is poetic and may be a quotation from some well-known proverb altered by James to stress **from above.** To say God gives such good things, of course, is to deny that he gives evil things, for the two are incompatible.

Yet James may intend a deeper truth than "God is good." He has already stated that God is a gracious giver with respect to all who ask (1:5). The chief good being asked in that context is wisdom, which in 3:15 will again be referred to, this time using the same term that occurs here (**from above**). Thus the best gift of all, referred to repeatedly in James, is wisdom, which helps one in the test. Therefore the deeper message is: God does not send the test; he gives the good gift of wisdom that enables us to stand in the test. He gives the antidote, not the poison.

Furthermore, the character of God is not subject to change. He is **the Father of the heavenly lights.** The reference is to creation, and it (and the one to the new creation in the next verse) indicates the extent of God's goodness. The lights of Genesis 1:18, that is, the sun and moon, were placed there for humanity's good. But this fact in turn suggests a contrast. The sun and moon were notorious for **change like shifting shadows** (not the best translation, for while James' language it obscure it is an astronomical phrase referring to the lack of constancy in the heavenly "lights"), but God, by way of contrast, has no eclipse, no rising and setting, no phases, no obscurity due to clouds. His character is absolutely constant, trustworthy, and dependable.

1:18 / As proof of God's goodwill—as if creation itself were not sufficient—James asserts, **He chose to give us birth through the word of truth**. First, what God did, he did by choice. His action was not an accident or a response to necessity. He chose, and therefore the action shows the essence of his character.

Second, **he** gave **us birth**. On the one hand, this action is creation. The Father of Lights is also the Father of Humanity and has willed all human life. On the other hand, not only did God produce creation, but he also produced new creation: He has produced the new birth or redemption in all believers (John 3:3–8; Rom. 12:2; Eph. 1:5; Titus 3:5; 1 Pet. 1:3, 23; 1 John 3:9). This statement produces a startling contrast: Desire brings to birth, but it bears sin and death; God brings to birth redemption and life.

Third, God does this new act of creation **through the word of truth**. This expression might at first glance be thought a reference to the creative word of God (Gen. 1) or to the veracity of all he says (e.g., Ps. 119:43), but surely in this passage something more is meant. What word in the New Testament era was more "the word of truth" than the gospel? The phrase is a semitechnical one designating the proclamation of God's action in Christ (2 Cor. 6:7; Eph. 1:18; Col. 1:5; 2 Tim. 2:15; 1 Pet. 1:25). God purposely sets his second creation, his re-creation, into motion by sending out the word of the gospel.

The result of this act is also beneficent, **that we might be a kind of firstfruits of all he created**. "We," says James, "are like a harvest. We are the first ripe fruit of God's new creation, promising the full harvest to come." Like Paul, James believes God will redeem all of creation, not just humanity (Rom. 8:18–25). The present rebirth of believers promises more to come. But the first are the best, the specially holy portion. Thus James underlines God's good gift and intention in the lives of the Christians.

1:19 / Deliberately paralleling the style of 1:16, James warns, **My dear brothers, take note of this.** James 1:16–18 discussed wisdom as a gift of life descending from God (cf. 1:5–8); now comes the related topic—the wise person controls his or her speech (cf. 3:1–18), for speech-ethics were a very important topic in both Jewish literature and the world in which James lived. James continues with a proverb: **Everyone should be quick to listen, slow to speak and slow to become angry.** As shocking as this saying is to this modern age of express-your-feelings, it was accepted wisdom in the biblical period: "He who guards his lips guards his life, but he who speaks rashly will come to ruin" (Prov. 13:3). "Do you see a man who speaks in haste? There is more hope for a fool than for him" (Prov. 29:20). "Do not get upset quickly, for anger resides in the lap of fools" (Eccles. 7:9). The truly wise and godly person in scripture is not the one who always has something to say but the person who listens to others, prayerfully considers, and only then speaks in measured tones.

James thinks of this proverb not just as a personal truth for each Christian but also as part of his concern for communal harmony. In 3:1 he points to conflicts among teachers that in 3:13–18 can lead to party spirit and jealousy. These were well known in the early church, encouraged by those drunk with the heady wine of the newly outpoured Spirit and preoccupied with *their* gift or ministry rather than the good of the church. James counsels caution and listening rather than quick speech and sharp denunciation.

1:20 / But what of righteous indignation? **Man's anger does not bring about the righteous life that God desires.** James never states his reason for this statement, but several appear in the New Testament. First, once the angry feeling begins to be expressed, it is by nature immoderate and uncontrollable, which made even Hellenistic pagan writers condemn anger. Second, anger is incompatible with the teaching of Jesus, particularly his command to love one's enemy (Matt. 5:38–48) and his direct condemnation of hating one's brother (Matt. 5:21–26). Third, hu-

man anger usurps the role of God as the only judge and vin-
dicator. In 5:7–9 James will indicate that the Christian is to wait
for *God's* vindication, not vindicate himself. A similar note is
sounded in Hebrews 10:30–39, Romans 12:19, and repeatedly in
1 Peter. The proper response to suffering is meekness and endurance, for God is the only true judge. Thus human anger cannot **bring about the righteous life that God desires**, either in the
sense of bringing about the righteousness God will establish in
the final day (which may be in mind here; cf. 5:7–11) or in the
sense of meeting God's present standard of righteousness. One
need only to reflect on Moses' impulsive murder of the Egyptian
taskmaster (Exod. 2:11–16) to discover a fine illustration of this
principle.

**1:21 / Therefore, get rid of all moral filth and the evil
that is so prevalent**. This clause is negative; the stress of the verse
is clearly on the positive (**accept the word**), but the negative is
the necessary prelude. Unless one recognizes sin for what it is,
ceases justifying it, and decisively rejects it, further progress is
unlikely. Thus in **get rid** James uses a term for conversion, picturing it like the removal of a soiled garment. The **moral filth** may
be any moral evil, especially greediness. But he focuses on anger,
or evil in speech, in **the evil that is so prevalent** (better translated
"every trace of malice" or "the malice which is so abundant").
Not just outward anger, but also all malice, is to be ruthlessly
chased from the heart.

With malice out, they can **accept the word that he plants
in your hearts**. These people have received the "word" of the gospel, for they are members of the Christian community. But the
word already planted in their hearts must be acted upon or accepted if it is to save them. It is not enough to be convinced about
Jesus; one must commit oneself to Jesus and his teaching, and
such a commitment is the changed lifestyle James is seeking.

In making this commitment they **humbly** submit to God.
James wrote in Greek "in meekness," indicating a submission to
God as opposed to the self-aggrandizement that quick speech and
anger demonstrate. Meekness is itself a fruit of the Spirit (Gal.
5:23; James 3:13) and a mark of those who will receive the Kingdom (Matt. 5:5). In this context it is a call to humble oneself before

God and accept God's way of leaving vengeance to him, to not reject the gospel teaching and take vengeance into one's own hands. This humble acceptance of the teaching of Jesus has a saving effect.

1:22 / The topic of accepting or obeying the word shifts James from the idea of speech to that of charitable action. **Do not merely listen to the word, and so deceive yourselves** refers to the person who is self-congratulatory about knowledge of scripture or mastery of the apostolic traditions about Jesus. It is not that such persons failed to *learn* the word of the apostolic teaching. They may be learned in scripture and accurate "scribes" of the teaching of Jesus. But they are **merely** listening. No matter how extensive one's scriptural knowledge, how amazing one's memory, it is self-deception if that is all there is.

Do what it says is the critical point. It is not what one knows, but what one does that counts. True knowledge is the prelude to action, and it is the obedience to the word that counts in the end.

1:23–24 / Having stated his thesis in the previous verse, James illustrates the *merely listening* position with a metaphor from daily life. It is like someone who carefully examines his or her face in a mirror in the morning. The beard is trimmed, the hair carefully combed into place, or the make-up applied. For the moment looking at his or her human face is an absorbing occupation. But once the morning ablutions are complete, no more thought is given to the matter; the person immediately **forgets what he looks like**, often operating during the day on the basis of a self-image at odds with his or her physical reality. If that is where it ends with scripture, all one's learning about the Bible or theology has exactly as much value for one's life as that morning facial examination.

1:25 / **But the [person] who looks intently . . . and continues to do this . . . will be blessed in what he does.** James makes the contrast two ways. First, the blessed person acts on what he or she knows rather than being one to **forget what he has heard,** the forgetting being not a loss from memory but a failure to live the teaching in the practical situation. James repeats the point, saying the person puts it into practice and that he or she is blessed **in what he does**. Action receives the accent. Second, the blessed person **continues to do this**. The theme of continuing, enduring, or remaining also occurs in James 1:2–4; 1:12; and 5:7–11. It is not the person who momentarily notices and obeys a command of Christ who will be blessed, but the person who is characterized by obedience to Christ's commands—for whom they are a chosen lifestyle. Such a person will indeed **be blessed in what he does**.

This "doer" studies **the perfect law that gives freedom**. By this James means not the Stoic rule of reason or the Jewish law, but the Jewish scriptures as interpreted and completed by the teaching of Jesus. In other words, **the perfect law** is the teaching of traditions from Jesus such as those embodied in the Sermon on the Mount (e.g., Matt. 5:17). Paul and James both agree that the teaching of Jesus is binding on the Christian and that no other way marks out the path of blessing and salvation. **Freedom** is not license but the ability to live and to fulfill "the law of Christ" (Gal. 6:2; cf. Gal. 5:13; 1 Cor. 9:21; 1 Cor. 7:10, 25—in the latter two verses a teaching of Christ ends discussion for Paul). This law is freeing, in that by submitting to Christ one is freed from bondage to sin and death, including all legalism (in the sense of meriting one's salvation). Thus James is saying that it is the person who *lives* this freedom who will be blessed by God, not the person who only *learns* about it.

1:26 / James has completed his opening statement. All that remains is to sum up in such a way that a transition is made to the next section. Verses 26–27 are that summary and transition.

If anyone considers himself religious . . . That is, does a person believe him- or herself to be a good, pious Christian? The focus is on religious performance, probably including such acts as worship, prayer and fasting, and systematic giving. James does not condemn the activities, but adds, **and yet does not keep a tight rein on his tongue, he deceives himself and his religion is worthless**. In other words, religious practices are fine, but if they are not coupled to an ethical lifestyle they are worse than useless, for they become self-deceptions. James' specific concern is the control of the tongue, by which he means angry outbursts, criticism, and complaining (cf. 1:19; 3:1, 13; 4:11–12; and 5:9). Criticism, judging, and gossiping reveal hearts not yet submitted to the rule of Christ. These are people whose overt religious practices, however Christian, are no more salvific than idolatry, also called **worthless** in scripture (Acts 14:15; 1 Cor. 3:20; 1 Pet. 1:18). James, like Jesus (Mark 12:28–34; John 13:34) and the prophets (Hos. 6:6; Isa. 1:1–10; Jer. 7:21–28), ruthlessly unmasks such self-deception so that his readers can recognize their true condition before it is too late.

1:27 / In contrast to the pious person with the sharp tongue, the religion that **God our Father** considers **pure and faultless** is not primarily ritual and pious practices but **looking after orphans and widows in their distress** and **keeping oneself from being polluted by the world**. The first characteristic, that of active charity and concern for the helpless and weak, is frequently mentioned in the Old Testament (Deut. 14:29; 24:17–22) as well as the New (Acts 6:1–6; 1 Tim. 5:3–16). The orphan and widow, along with the foreigner and Levite, formed the traditional poor of early Israel. True piety, then, will help the weak, the poor, for God is the helper of the helpless (Deut. 10:16–17).

The second characteristic focuses on the world, a designation common in Paul and John for human culture, mores, and institutions (1 Cor. 1–3; 5:19; Eph. 2:2; John 12:31; 15:18–17:16; 1 John 2:15–17). True piety is not conformity to human culture but transformation into Christ's image (Rom. 12:1–2). For James this means specifically rejecting the motives of competition, personal ambition, and accumulation that lie at the root of a lack of charity and an abundance of community conflict (e.g., 4:1–4). In declaring this alone to be true religion in *God's* eyes, James declares that conversion is meaningless unless it leads to a changed life.

Additional Notes §1

1:1 / **The twelve tribes** of Israel were God's chosen people in the Old Testament. James looks on the church as the continuation of that people of God. The church includes the remnant of the old Israel and takes into itself the converts from the Gentiles. It is therefore "the Israel of God" (Gal. 6:16), the people of God in the new age of the Spirit (cf. Rom 4:13–25; Gal. 5:21–31).

Scattered among the nations is a technical term for the dispersion or Diaspora. After the exile of Jews from Palestine in 586 B.C., most did not return. Instead they spread out through the cities of Asia and Europe, westward to Rome and Spain, south to Egypt, and east to Babylon and Persia. To the Jews living in Palestine, these people were Diaspora, scattered people, exiles from the land to which they belonged. James uses this term for Christians, for they are also "exiles" in the land in which they live. In much the same way, Peter refers to Christians as sojourners or pilgrims (1 Pet. 1:1, 17; 2:11).

1:2 / The phrase **consider it pure joy** has as its central word the Greek word "joy," *charan*, which forms a wordplay with the *chairein*, "greetings" of v. 1. James uses such wordplay links to tie his letter together despite his tendency to juxtapose topics.

The structure of vv. 2–4 is that of a chain saying, which is also found in Rom. 5:3–5 and 1 Pet. 1:6–7. In 1 Peter, in particular, some identical phrases are used. The saying appears to have been widely and loosely used within the early church, which means that each author felt free to adapt it to make his own point. The basis of the structure is probably some statement of Jesus similar to that in Matt. 5:11–12, "Happy are you when men insult you. Rejoice and be glad, because a great reward is kept for you in heaven." For further reading see D. Daube, *The New Testament and Rabbinic Judaism*, pp. 113, 117–19.

The idea of **trials** is not a new idea to the readers of this letter, for it is deeply rooted in Judaism. The earliest reference is in Gen. 22:1, an incident referred to in James 2:21, where God tests Abraham. God is also said to test the Israelites in the wilderness, but unlike Abraham they fail the test (Num. 14:20–24). As one moves into the intertestamental period, one finds the famous reference in Sirach 2:1–6:

> My son, when thou comest to serve the Lord, prepare thy soul for temptation. Set thy heart aright and endure firmly, and be not fearful in time of calamity. . . . Accept whatsoever is brought upon thee, and be patient in disease and poverty. For gold is proved in the fire, and men acceptable to God in the furnace of affliction.

(Cf. Jubilees 8:25, or the Dead Sea Scrolls 1 QS 10, 17, 1 QH 5:15–17; 1 QM 16:15–17:3). Thus the early church had a long tradition upon which to draw that expected faith to be tested. See H. Seesemann *"Peira,"* *TDNT,* vol. 6, pp. 23–26, for further data.

1:3 / The phrase **the testing of your faith** is a single word in Greek, *dokimion*. It properly refers to the means of testing in this passage, although in 1 Pet. 1:7 it refers to the result of the test, i.e., genuineness. The means, however unpleasant they may be, produce a good result. They are not simply negative, destroying ungenuine faith, but positive, if viewed in the right light.

The term **perseverance**, Greek *hypomonē*, is virtually a technical term in the New Testament. Paul uses the term sixteen times (2 Cor. 6:4; 12:12; 1 Thess. 1:3), and Revelation finds it most important (1:9; 2:2; 13:10; 14:12). It is obvious, from this fact and the fact that its use for Abraham, Job, etc., is found in intertestamental works, that the virtue is important in a community suffering persecution. The Jews after the exile, and particularly after the persecution by Antiochus Epiphanes (167–164 B.C.) were concerned about holding fast to the faith despite opposition, disadvantage, or even persecution. They looked to the Old Testament to supply examples, which they exegeted accordingly. Likewise the church found itself vulnerable as a despised and persecuted minority within Judaism and, later, the Roman Empire. Fly-by-night or flash-in-the-pan Christianity would not do. It is not those who apostasize and fall away but "he who endures to the end" who will be saved (Mark 13:13; Matt. 10:22; 24:13). Thus endurance is one of the cardinal virtues of the Christian life, not a side issue. To endure means to copy Christ in his endurance and to assure oneself of future blessedness.

1:4 / The term **must finish its work** is literally "have its perfect [or complete] work." It is this phraseology that suggested to many commentators that a specific virtue is in mind. Instead of a single virtue, however, *"You* are that perfect work" (M. Dibelius, *James,* p. 74).

The idea of perfection is not original in James. Noah is the archetypal perfect person: "Noah was a righteous man, perfect in his generation" (Gen. 6:9). He kept God's law, or he was "of stable integrity, not contaminated by divergent motives or conflicts between thoughts and deeds" (P. J. DuPlessis, *Telios: The Idea of Perfection in the New Testament,* pp. 94–99). Thus the people of the Dead Sea Scrolls could both think of themselves as perfect because of their inward and outward dedication to God (1 QS 2:1–2; 14:7; 1 QH 1:36) and still long for a higher perfection (1 QS 4:20–22). For Paul, Christians are also already the perfect or mature (1 Cor. 2:6), but becoming perfect or mature people is still a process going on with its goal in the future (Eph. 4:13; cf. Col. 4:12; Phil. 3:15). For Matthew, as in the Dead Sea Scrolls, perfection consists in copying God (*imitatio dei,* Matt. 5:48), but in both Matthew and Paul this was re-interpreted in terms of a more available example, God-in-Flesh, Jesus. Thus it becomes copying Christ (*imitatio Christi,* Matt. 19:21; cf. Phil.

2:5ff.). Perfection, then, is a tension. It is both possible and impossible, both present and future. See further, W. D. Davies, *The Setting of the Sermon on the Mount*, pp. 212–13; and R. Schippers, "Goal," *NIDNTT*, vol. 2, pp. 59–66. The important fact to consider is the eschatological nature of perfection, its "now" and "not yet" tension, as well as the fact that in its realizable form it is focused on copying God and Christ and thus needs divine revelation and human obedience.

1:5 / The English wordplay lacking (v. 4)–lacks (v. 5) is also present in Greek. This catchword linking of ideas is a favorite method by which James joins them into a unity.

The idea of **wisdom** in James is not simply insight or God's law (as in Sirach 4:17; Wisdom 7:15; 8:21) but a gift of the coming new age that can now be found in those who belong to that age (as in 2 Baruch 44:14; 2 Esdras 8:52; 1 Enoch 5:8; 98:1–9; 100:6). As these Jewish parallels (and others in the Dead Sea Scrolls: 1 QS 11; CD 2; 6:3; 11 Q Psa 154) show, Jewish readers would recognize a tension. Wisdom will only be fully possessed in the coming age, but the righteous remnant ("the wise" of Dan. 11–12) already have a foretaste of it in this age. It is this that leads people to perfection, a relationship between wisdom and perfection that Paul also recognized (1 Cor. 2:4–6). See J. A. Kirk, "The Meaning of Wisdom in James."

God is a good giver (Prov. 3:23; cf. Didache 4:7; Hermas *Mandate* 9), but he is also a generous giver (Hermas *Mandate* 2). The term for generosity, *haplos*, appears in the New Testament only here. It is related to the term *haplotēs*, which means sincerity. Epictetus shows the meaning of *haplos* when he writes, "Stop letting yourself be drawn this way and that . . . but be either this or that *simply* and with all your mind" (*Discourses* II, 2, 13). The same sense of simplicity and sincerity is to be in human giving according to Jesus, for in a context on giving he says, "If your eyes are clear [*haplotēs*], your whole body will be full of light" (Matt. 6:22), which is an idiom for sincere giving, as bad eyes were for stinginess. On this term see further B. Gärtner, "Simplicity," *NIDNTT*, vol. 3, pp. 571-72.

1:6 / "Faith" has far more than one meaning in James. Here and in 1:3, 2:5, and 5:15, it means commitment, trust; in 2:14–26 it means intellectual assent; and in 2:1 it means the body of truth about Jesus that is believed. This first use is most like Paul; the others differ from Paul's. See O. Michel, "Faith," *NIDNTT*, vol. 1, pp. 587–606.

To **doubt** shows that the person is unlike God. God gives sincerely, with an undivided mind. The doubter prays, but without an undivided mind. He is not at all certain God will answer. The figure of the swaying **wave** was popular in Jewish and Greek literature, e.g., Sirach 33:1-3:

> No evil befalls the man who fears the Lord, but in trial he will deliver him again and again. A wise man will not hate the law, but he who is hypocritical about it is like a boat in a storm. A man of understanding will trust in the law.

1:7–8 / The chief term in these verses is *dipsychos*, translated as **double-minded**. The term itself is found first in James and may have been coined by the author. The idea, however, has deep Jewish roots. A person is to seek God with his or her whole heart (Deut. 6:5; 18:3), and thus to doubt or have a **double** heart is in itself evil, a mark of hypocrisy (Ps. 12:1–2; 1 Chron. 12:33). Jewish tradition was constantly calling people to a clear choice: It cannot be God *and* Baal or God *and* Egypt; it must be either one or the other. The sharp contrast continues in Sirach (e.g., 33:7–15) and later literature. Testament of Levi 13:1 calls, "Fear the Lord your God with your whole heart, and walk in simplicity according to all his Law." One notices how simplicity (*haplotēs* from James 1:5) is important. Testament of Benjamin 6:5 adds, "The good mind hath not two tongues, of blessing and of cursing . . . of hypocrisy and of truth . . . ; but it hath one disposition, uncorrupt and pure, concerning all men." The people at Qumran were likewise concerned lest someone who had outwardly (and perhaps meaning it at the time) pledged to follow the way of God would turn back and follow his or her evil nature to the detriment of the community:

> No man shall walk in the stubbornness of his heart so that he strays after his heart and eyes and evil inclination, but he shall circumcise in the Community the foreskin of evil inclination and of stiffness of neck that they may lay a foundation of truth for Israel, for the community of the everlasting Council (1 QS 5:4–5).

People who did turn back were surely condemned:

> As for them, they dissemble,
>   they plan devilish schemes.
> They seek Thee with a double heart
>   and are not confirmed in Thy truth.
> A root bearing poisoned and bitter fruit
>   is in their designs;
> they walk in stubbornness of heart
>   and seek Thee among idols,
> and they set before them
>   the stumbling-block of their sin.
>   (1 QH 4:13–14)

Paul has a similar concern, although expressed in less colorful language, in Romans 6–8. People might commit to Christ but then "walk after the flesh." Paul reacts to the idea with horror. By no means should such instability be allowed. Single-hearted devotion to God is the order of the day.

James' concern with a double heart and instability was later picked up by Hermas (*Mandate* 9 for *dipsychos* and *Mandate* 2.3 and 5.2.7 for *instability*, which Hermas considers demonic in origin). But the idea is weakened there. James uses it with the full force of tradition. Hermas has concern simply about effective prayer.

1:9 / James does not use the usual term for poor, *ptōchos*, but *tapeinos*, which in other contexts means humble or socially low or unimportant (2 Cor. 7:6; 10:1). In this context it clearly means materially poor because of its contrast with rich. *Tapeinos* appears multiple times in the Septuagint (the Greek translation of the Old Testament) for six different Hebrew terms meaning poor or oppressed. It is especially suitable, because of its dual connotation of humble and poor, to translate *'ani*, a frequent Hebrew term for the humble poor (perhaps behind Matt. 5:3 as well). It is also interesting that it appears in Prov. 3:34, since James will later quote this verse (4:6); it may already be on his mind. See also Judg. 6:15; Pss. 9:39; 33:18; Amos 8:6; Isa. 11:4, and W. Grundmann, *"Tapeinos,"* in *TDNT*, vol. 8, pp. 1–26.

The term **ought to take pride** is the Greek verb *kauchaomai*, which outside of its use here and in 4:16 is always used in the New Testament by Paul (thirty-five times). Normally this verb means pride or boasting in a negative sense and is thus hardly a command to the Christian (Gal. 6:13; Rom. 2:23; 1 Cor. 1:29; 2 Cor. 5:12; Eph. 2:9). In the Old Testament, however, one could boast in God (Pss. 32:11; 149:5). This positive sense is taken over by Paul when he speaks of boasting in God or in Christ (Rom. 5:11; 1 Cor. 1:31; Phil. 3:3). It is this positive sense that James intends, for to be glad or to boast in one's exaltation is to boast, not about one's own works, but about what God has done for one. Thus it is a form of boasting in God. It is therefore interesting that Paul uses this verb in Rom. 5:3; a passage parallel to James 1:2 and 1 Pet. 1:6. This shows that in Paul's mind the positive sense of boasting is close to the eschatological joy expressed by James and Peter in their respective terms. The idea of such joy will appear three times in this one chapter in James (1:2; 1:9; 1:12).

1:10 / James has two ways of handling **rich** persons. First, he refers to them using the term *plousios*. In these three instances they are unbelievers, opposers of the gospel (1:10; 2:6; 5:1ff.). Second, he refers to them using circumlocutions that describe them but never call them rich (2:2; 4:13). In these cases, the people are wealthier members of the Christian community. In contrast, the term "poor" (*ptōchos*) is at times in James a name for the community, following Jewish usage for the remnant of Israel (e.g., Psalms of Solomon).

The idea that the rich will be brought low and the poor exalted is a familiar reversal-of-fortunes theme. One encounters it in the Old Testament (1 Sam. 2:7) and frequently in the psalms (e.g., Pss. 37; 73) as well as in Luke's Magnificat (Luke 1:53). A similar theme occurs in 1 Enoch. More importantly, the Lukan beatitudes express it clearly (Luke 6:20-26):

20Looking at his disciples, he said:
"Blessed are you who are poor,
for yours is the kingdom of God.
21Blessed are you who hunger now,
for you will be satisfied.
Blessed are you who weep now,
for you will laugh.

²²Blessed are you when men hate you, when they exclude you and insult you and reject your name as evil, because of the Son of Man. ²³"Rejoice in that day and leap for joy, because great is your reward in heaven. For that is how their fathers treated the prophets.

²⁴"But woe to you who are rich,
     for you have already received your comfort.
²⁵Woe to you who are well fed now,
     for you will go hungry.
Woe to you who laugh now,
     for you will mourn and weep.
Woe to you when all men speak well of you,
     for that is how their fathers treated the false prophets."

The wealthy have absolutely nothing to rejoice about. Like the rich man in the parable (Luke 16:19–31), they are on their way to hell. James is here applying this teaching and exhorting his congregation to act on it.

1:11 / The picture is an image that is very widespread. One sees it in Testament of Job 33 and in Pliny, *Natural History* 21, 1. It occurs in Ps. 103:15–16, which, along with Isa. 40:6, might be in James' mind, and in Matt. 6:30 and Luke 12:28 (although with a different application). Though it is especially suited to Palestine, other warm climates would also find the expression meaningful.

Some scholars have seen **with scorching heat** (*kausoni*) as indicating the sirocco, or hot desert wind, as in Job 27:21; Jer. 18:17; and Hos. 12:1. In fact, it may well be referred to in Ps. 103:16. But this is unlikely (although tempting, for the sirocco is distinctly Palestinian), for the sirocco has nothing to do with **the sun** rising. It blows constantly day and night for the whole period of its effect. Thus James' description is best seen as a proverbial reference to the sun's withering activity in warm, dry climates.

The rich person is **destroyed**. The verb *maranthesetai* literally means "to wither" and is applied to the withering of plants and, metaphorically, the death of persons. One might think, then, that this is simply a reference to the impermanence of the rich. They will die and all their deeds will crumble. But James is probably thinking on a deeper level, as Jesus does in Luke 12:16–21. The person not only faces the **sun** of life's troubles but the **scorching heat** of God's judgment (as 5:1–6 will show). The fading away is not simply a withering, but a destruction, an eternal fact that should strike terror in the hearts of all tempted to the same lifestyle.

1:12 / The term **blessed** (*makarios*) is also used in the Beatitudes and Psalms (e.g., Ps. 1). Its opposite is "woe."

The idea of **persever**ing (*hypomenō*) is very important in the New Testament (Matt. 10:22; 24:13; Mark 13:13; Rom. 12:12; 1 Cor. 13:7; 2 Tim. 2:12, etc., use the verb; Luke 21:19; Rom. 2:7; 8:25; 2 Cor. 6:4; 1 Thess. 1:3; Rev. 13:10, and twenty-six other passages use the noun, *hypomonē*). It was critical that Christians be taught to endure, or else the church would have vanished at the first approach of persecution. The virtue was also valued in some Jewish circles (e.g., Testament of Job and Testament of Joseph).

Paul uses the idea of standing **the test** five times (cf. also 2 Tim. 2:15). The adjective *dokimos* indicates human or divine approval and is what Paul hoped for himself at the last judgment. He, like James, never assumed this final approval until he arrived there (e.g., Phil. 3:12–16).

The idea of receiving **the crown of life** at the last judgment is expressed in identical language in Rev. 2:10 and in similar language ("the crown of glory") in 1 Pet. 5:4.

The promise to **those who love him** (cf. James 2:5) is nowhere explicitly stated in scripture, although its general sense is frequent enough (Exod. 20:5–6; 1 Cor. 2:9; Eph. 6:24). Some have argued that this verse cites an unrecorded saying of Jesus, which is possible, but not provable.

1:13 / When James denies that **God is tempting me** and asserts that **he does** not **tempt anyone**, he is following Judaism. Although early parts of the Old Testament could state without a qualm "God tests" (e.g., Abraham in Gen. 22:1 and David in 2 Sam. 24:1), after the exile Judaism found these statements too facile. Thus in 2 Chron. 21:1 the devil, not God, tests David; in Job the test is initiated and carried out by Satan, although God gives permission; and in Jubilees 17–19 the devil (Mastema) initiates and carries out the testing of Abraham. For James, God is sovereign, but it is other forces that will and cause evil.

One reason for James' dealing with the question may stem from the recitation of the Greek form of the Lord's Prayer, "Do not lead us into temptation, but deliver us from evil." In Greek it sounds as if God might be the agent of testing and as if one must beg for deliverance. Yet the Aramaic form of the prayer (and the applications in Luke 22:40) clearly shows the intention to be, "Cause that we not enter the test," which fits with "and deliver us from the Evil One." God is the one who *prevents the devil* from testing the Christian or sets limits on the extent of the test.

The retranslation **God cannot be tempted by evil** is a translation of "God is *apeirastos*." The problem is that *apeirastos* is a rare word that occurs first in James and then almost nowhere else in Greek literature. The translation preferred in this commentary, "God ought not to be tested by evil men," is based on the use of the word by the church fathers, the form of the word, and the Old Testament teaching that prohibits testing God. See further P. H. Davids, "The Meaning of *Apeirastos*," *NTS* 24 (1978), pp. 386–91. On the testing tradition in general see B. Gerhardsson, *The Testing of God's Son*.

1:14 / The citation of **desire** as the tempter draws upon a major Jewish tradition concerning the evil impulse in humanity (the evil *yēṣer* The *yēṣer* is simply undifferentiated desire, striving for whatever it sees. It is not the self or *ego* of the person (it fits more closely Freud's id), but unless it is limited by the Law or Torah (in Judaism) or some other counterforce, it will control the ego. Thus Paul sees himself as controlled by sin, the flesh, or the law of sin, despite his recognition of its evil nature and his approval of the law—for Paul Torah was not enough, it simply let one know how enslaved one really was (Rom. 7). Paul's answer is that the Spirit is the counterforce releasing one from desire/sin (Rom. 8). James will give a similar answer in his call for wisdom (1:17; 3:13–18, etc.). The important fact for him in this passage, as for the Jews, was that of personal responsibility. The person had to admit that he or she was to blame; sin rested in him or her, not in something external. Thus in the Christian tradition the Episcopal Church confessed, we are "miserable sinners . . . there is no health in us." For further discussion of the *yêṣer* tradition, see F. C. Porter, "The Yeser Hara: A Study in the Jewish Doctrine of Sin"; and G. F. Moore, *Judaism in the First Centuries of the Christian Era*, vol. 1, pp. 479–93.

1:15 / The picture of **desire** as an enticing woman may have been drawn from Proverbs. In Proverbs 1–9 wisdom appears as the good and holy woman who leads one to life and God. In chaps. 5 and 7 another woman appears, who entices and leads away those to whom wisdom is calling. She promises to fulfill their desires, but the end result is death. The use of the picture of the arrow and the snare in Prov. 7:22–23 is very appropriate in the context of James. Likewise the image of adultery is very appropriate, for the evil impulse is often connected to adultery in Jewish literature. Cf. S. Schechter, *Some Aspects of Rabbinic Theology*, p. 250.

Some authors see in this verse a reference to Jewish views of Satan's attack upon Eve or the soul, particularly in the sexual language (for Satan's seduction of Eve see 4 Macc. 18:7–8; Apocalypse of Moses 19:3; Testament of Reuben 2; and Testament of Benjamin 7). This reference is unlikely for the *female* (**desire**) is the aggressor here in the first case of birth, and in the second, no paternal figure is named. James, who wishes to stress personal responsibility, would hardly leave open the possibility of blaming both Satan and Eve for one's sin.

On the relationship of sin to the heart see E. Arnold, *Inner Land* (Rifton, N.Y.: Plough Publishers, 1976), esp. chap. 3, "The Heart."

The relationship of **sin** and **death** is abundantly clear in scripture: Gen. 2:17; Ezek. 18:4; Rom. 5:12 (also include Jesus' references to Gehenna and outer darkness, Revelation's to "the second death," and 1 John 5:16–17). That James sees this as more than physical death (the consequence of sin in 1 Cor. 11:30; 5:5; and 1 Tim. 1:20), is clear in James 5:19–20.

1:16 / The idea of deception (*planaō*) occurs frequently in scripture, not referring to a simple failure in judgment, but to serious deviation from the truth, which strikes at the heart of faith itself: Rom. 1:27; 1 Cor. 6:9; Gal. 6:7; 1 John 1:8; 4:6; 2 Pet. 2:18; 3:17; and frequently in Revelation. Cf. H. Braun, "*Planaō*," *TDNT*, vol. 6, pp. 242–51.

1:17 / The original quotation from which **every good and perfect gift** is taken may have been, "Every Gift is good and every present is perfect," which roughly translates "Don't look a gift horse in the mouth." James' change was simply to add **from above** or "from heaven," which altered the whole sense. Now, not people but God is the source of all perfect gifts. What God gives is not stated, but if our analysis of form is correct (Introduction, "Form"), then this is parallel to 1:5–8 and thus concerns wisdom, the best gift of all (as Luke 11:13), which is needed to counter the evil impulse of 1:2–4 and 1:12–15. The phrase added is frequently used to indicate the divine origin of God's Spirit or of faith (in contrast to demonic or earthly origin): John 3; Shepherd of Hermas *Mandate* 9.11; 11.5.

The phrase **Father of the heavenly lights** is literally "Father of lights." On the one hand this is a circumlocution. James, like a good Jew, avoids using the name of God where he does not feel it is necessary (as the rabbinic "The Holy One, blessed be he" rather than "God"). On the other hand, though this reflects James' belief that God created the stars (Gen. 1:14–18; Ps. 135:7; Jer. 4:23; 21:35), it may also reflect a belief that God is more personally related to them than that, that the stars and planets are, or are ruled by, animate beings or spirits (Job 38:7; 1 Enoch 18:12–16; 1 QS 3:20; etc.). The imagery is clearly that of Judaism and not of the Hellenistic world, which did not use "lights" to refer to heavenly bodies. See further G. F. Moore, *Judaism in the First Centuries of the Christian Era*, vol. 1, p. 403; and H. Conzelmann, "*Phōs*," *TDNT*, vol. 9, pp. 319–27.

The difficulty with the final phrase **does not change like shifting shadows** is partially a textual problem. It is obvious from the state of the Greek text that early copyists had problems in understanding exactly which phenomenon James had in mind: changing constellations, an eclipse, or nightfall. It was well known that the heavenly bodies changed (Sirach 17:31; 27:11; Wisdom 7:29; 1 Enoch 41; 72) and that God did not (Job 25:5). In fact, it was so well known that it is probably an error to ask James for too much precision about which phenomena he has in mind. The heavens change and are changed (darkened by the movements of other bodies). That fact contrasts clearly with their creator.

1:18 / This whole verse breathes creation language. For example, the participle (in Greek) **he chose** is in the emphatic position just as it is in Philo's works when referring to the creative desires of God. This fact has led some writers to argue that only the original creation of humanity is in mind, but the following language rules this out. Creation it is, but *new* creation (cf. 2 Cor. 5:17).

That God chose **to give us birth** has been problematic to some, for strictly speaking the verb applies only to the female act of giving birth. But two pieces of data resolve the problem: (1) Female imagery is sometimes applied to God in scripture (Num. 11:12; Deut. 32:8; Deut. 32:18a in the Septuagint; Pss. 7:14; 90:2; Isa. 66:13), and (2) James needed an action parallel to desire in 1:15.

Regeneration language (which is very close to the Johannine tradition, e.g., John 3–13, 1 John 3:9–10) and new creation language (which is closer to Paul, e.g., 2 Cor. 5:17, Rom. 8:18–25) come together in this passage. The imagery is very fluid.

In **that we might be a kind of firstfruits**, a new type of imagery, harvest imagery, appears. In the Old Testament the first fruits may designate either the temporal order of the event (Christ is the first raised, 1 Cor. 15:20; Stephanus the first saved, 1 Cor. 16:15; the Christians are the first redeemed, 2 Thess. 2:13) or the quality of the group (Rev. 14:4). Here the reference to creation emphasizes temporal priority: The rebirth of Christians begins the redemption of all creation. See further G. Delling, *"Haparchē," TDNT*, vol. 1, pp. 484–86.

1:19 / The proverb comes from a Jewish context, as its language indicates (**everyone** is *pas anthrōpos*, a Semitism), but its wisdom is not only found widely in Jewish sources (Prov. 15:1; Sirach 1:22; 4:29; 6:33; Psalms of Solomon 16:10; m. Aboth 2:10) but also in pagan sources (Dio Chrysostom 32 ["Don't be quick to anger but slow"]; Diogenes Laertius 8.23; Seneca *Ira*). In fact, so prevalent is the concern for controlled speech, including the control of anger, that W. R. Baker wrote a whole doctoral dissertation on this and other themes of speech-ethics as they relate to James (*Personal Speech-Ethics: a Study of the Epistle of James against its Background* [University of Aberdeen, 1986]). The one major difference between James (and other New Testament writers) and Jewish (including the Old Testament) and pagan writers on the topic is that James and the New Testament do not recommend silence, perhaps due to the urgency of spreading the gospel.

For anger, noise, and party strife in the New Testament, 1 Cor. 14; 1 Thess. 5:19–22; and 1 Tim. 1:3ff. are examples. See also the parties of 1 Cor. 1–3. It is not necessary to posit political agitation or Zealotism, as Bo Reicke does (*James*, p. 21), to find a setting for this proverb's use in James' community.

1:20 / **Anger**, usually meaning the *expression* of hostility, was rejected by the Greeks, as H. Kleinknecht shows (*"Orgē," TDNT*, vol. 5, p. 384). Later Jewish writers rejected it as incompatible with wisdom (Sirach 27:30; Wisdom 10:3; cf. Job 36:13; 18; Prov. 12:16; 27:3; 4; 29:8; 30:33). In Christian literature not only does the Sermon on the Mount reject anger using the same term as James does (Matt. 5:22), but anger is frequently included in lists of vices (Eph. 4:31; Col. 3:8). Prayer is incompatible with anger (1 Tim. 2:8). Ephesians 4:26 (quoting Ps. 4:4) indicates that Paul did not want one to repress anger but to admit the emotion and sublimate it (e.g., through confrontation and reconciliation, forgiveness, or prayer) "before the sun sets." Repressing it only makes an explosion more likely. See further H. C. Hahn, "Anger," *NIDNTT*, vol. 1, pp. 105–13.

1:21 / **Get rid** is a participle in Greek, clearly subordinate to the main verb, **accept**, although it precedes it in time. The word is frequently used in Christian literature for a change of lifestyle, e.g., Eph. 4:22; 1 Pet. 2:1; 1 Clement 13:1.

The word **moral filth** is used more outside the New Testament than within (e.g., in Epictetus or Philo). See further J. I. Packer, "Dirt, Filth, Refuse," *NIDNTT*, vol. 1, p. 479.

The phrase **the evil that is so prevalent** may mean "a large amount of wickedness," "a large amount of malice," or very possibly "every trace or remainder of malice." The key to this latter translation is that the *perisseu* stem is often used in the Old Testament to translate the Hebrew *ytr* root, which means either abundance or remainder.

God has im**planted** the word. Some have argued that this means "innate" or "inborn," as it often does in Hellenistic literature. However, not only early Christian teaching (Barnabas 1:2; 9:9) but also the biblical tradition thinks of God's word, or the gospel, as implanted by God in one's heart at conversion (Deut. 30:1; Matt. 13:4–15, 18–23; 1 Cor. 3:6; 1 Thess. 1:6; 2:13). It is this sense that fits best here. As in the parable of the sower, the word may be planted, but unless obeyed it is soon choked, with fatal results.

The phrase **in you** (cf. GNB, "in your hearts") is a correct interpretation of the normal biblical location of such implantation, but in some translations the following phrase is "save your soul." The salvation James refers to is a deliverance from the apocalyptic judgment of God in the last day. "Souls" is correctly interpreted in the NIV as simply **you**, for *psychē* means the whole person or self (cf. Deut. 6:5; Job 33:28; Mark 8:35; John 10:11; Acts 2:41).

For the virtue of meekness, see further F. Hauck and S. Schulz, *"Praus," TDNT*, vol. 6, pp. 645–51.

1:22 / The background of this verse is the Old Testament idea of doing the law (Deut. 28:53; 29:28; cf. 1 Macc. 2:16; Sirach 19:20). The teaching of Jesus was the new law for the Christian community (Rom. 8:2; 1 Cor. 9:21; Gal. 6:2). The saying itself can be duplicated in Jewish sources: "Not the expounding of the law is the chief thing but the doing of it" (m. *Aboth* 1:17) or "You ought not only to read the laws of Moses, but rather to practice what they command you" (Josephus, *Antiquities* 20.44). Jesus has a similar saying in Matt. 7:21–27 (Luke 6:46–49), leading Origen (*Homily* on Gen. 2:16) to believe this verse to be an otherwise unrecorded saying of Jesus.

The term for to **deceive yourselves** occurs in Col. 2:4 and other parallels where it means to lead one from the faith. Thus the hearers only deceive themselves about their salvation.

The term *listener* in **listen to the word** does not refer to a casual listener but is the regular classical Greek term for a serious auditor or pupil (e.g., Plato, *Republic* 536c; Aristotle, *Politics* 1274).

1:23–24 / The mirror metaphor is used elsewhere in scripture and intertestamental literature (1 Cor. 13:12; Sirach 12:11; Wisdom 7:26), as well as other Greek literature, but these uses have no relationship to James. Copper or bronze mirrors were too common household items not to have been frequently chosen as illustrations.

Some commentators argue the terms **looks . . . in a mirror** and **looking at himself** mean to "glance at" as opposed to a more careful look at the law in v. 25 (e.g., J. Adamson, *James*, p. 82). But not only does this not fit James' point, it also makes a false assertion about the Greek term (cf. Matt. 7:23; Luke 12:27; Luke 20:3). See further S. S. Laws, *James*, p. 86; and J. Goetzmann, "Reason," *NIDNTT*, vol. 3, p. 126.

1:25 / The term **blessed** (*makarios*) turns attention to the previous use of the word in 1:12. As in Matt. 5:3–9 (and with a background in Ps. 1:1; Isa. 56:2, etc.) the blessing is not temporal prosperity but future approval, or joy when the kingdom of God is fully established (cf. 5:7–11).

The perfect law that gives freedom has been frequently discussed. The Stoic use of the term (e.g., Epictetus 4.1.158) is discussed by J. Blunk, "Freedom," *NIDNTT*, vol. 1, pp. 715–16, and H. Schlier, "*Eleutheros*," *TDNT*, vol. 2, pp. 493–96. Philo attempted to apply this idea to the Mosaic Law as being true reason (e.g., *Vita Moesis* 2.48). On the other hand, there is no evidence of the Stoic idea in James other than this verbal similarity, and there is abundant evidence that the Jews of all types saw their law as perfect and freeing (Pss. 119; 19:7–11; 40:6–8; Rom. 7:12; m. *Aboth* 3:5; 6:2). W. D. Davies, *The Setting of the Sermon on the Mount*, has shown that the Jews expected Messiah to reinterpret the law. This Jewish expectation is precisely what early Christians saw Jesus fulfilling, giving the new and perfect law for the new age (cf. Barnabas 2:6 and Hermas *Vision* 1.3).

1:26 / **Religion** or **religious** is not commonly used in scripture, the adjective occurring in the Greek Bible only here and the noun only in v. 27; Acts 26:5; and Col. 2:18 in the New Testament. The terms refer to the religious performance either positively or negatively.

The idea of **worthless**ness occurs again in 2:14–26, where faith that does not produce action is declared unable to save.

1:27 / The terms **pure and faultless** or "pure and unblemished" are also found in Didache 1:5 and Hermas *Mandate* 2.7; *Similitude* 5.7.1. They are probably an idiom for absolute purity.

The reference to God as **Father** is not unusual for James (1:17; 3:9), but here it may stress God as the universal Father who is the father to orphans and husband to the widow. This allusion would make the demand for charity flow out of God's nature.

The **world** is referred to here in a distinctly Christian sense, as H. Sasse, "*Kosmos*," *TDNT*, vol. 3, pp. 889–95, points out. The only Jewish passages that reject human culture in this same way are suspected of Christian influence (e.g., 1 Enoch 48:7; 108:8). For Christians, the world could **pollute**, or spot, them. Thus it was imperative to remain unspotted, which was originally a cultic term for purity and acceptability for cultic service (i.e., temple worship; cf. 1 Pet. 1:19) but now has taken on a moral tone (as in 1 Tim. 6:14; 2 Pet. 3:14).

§2 *Prejudice and the Poor (James 2:1–26)*

In chapter 2 James expands upon the theme of worldliness and the care of widows. Worldliness shows up not only as personal ambition but also in a church's paying regard to someone's worldly power and position rather than dealing only on the basis of that person's spiritual position in Christ. This issue, in turn, leads to the statement of the need for generosity and to a warning against a complacent orthodoxy that stops short of gospel obedience (2:14–26).

2:1 / **My brothers** recognizes the readers' status as church members. **Don't show favoritism:** Despite the fact that God shows no partiality (Deut. 10:17; Gal. 2:6), human beings who serve under his authority and supposedly copy his character must be continually warned against being partial (e.g., Deut. 1:17; Lev. 19:15; Ps. 82:2; Prov. 6:35; 18:5). A glance at who is elected to office in the church and who sits on denominational committees would quickly indicate that despite the very negative view Jesus took of wealth (e.g., Mark 10), James' reproof is still relevant today. The church ought to show no partiality, no concern about the outward beauty, wealth, or power of a person.

This is demanded of us **as believers in our glorious Lord Jesus Christ.** The only basis of the church is faith in a single Lord. Belief and commitment save rich and poor alike, and all pledge allegiance to a Lord whose life and teaching ignored, if not despised, worldly position. Furthermore, this Lord is living, exalted, glorious; he will return to manifest his glory and judge the world. Partiality is a violation of his character and an insult to him; it is therefore a serious sin.

2:2–4 / Having stated his topic, James gives an example based on realistic (even if hypothetical) events in the church. **Suppose a man comes into your meeting wearing a gold ring and**

fine clothes: The words describe a person walking in, neatly dressed in clean (lit., "shining") clothes. The gold ring on his finger announces his wealth. One can feel the uneasy deference of the group already present. Next, **a poor man in shabby clothes also comes in**. He owns only one set of clothes, so they are filthy rags. Used to being rejected, he slinks in the door only to feel those assembled draw back from him as he expected; the trashy state of his clothes declares him to be human trash, of no value in worldly terms.

The church responds to the economic status of the rich man: **Here's a good seat for you**. He eases himself into the most comfortable chair, to the warm smiles of all present. The poor man, however, receives only a cold **You stand there**, or **Sit on the floor by my feet**. The room is crowded; let him reverence his betters by standing, or even sitting at their feet. Most of those present, of course, try not to even notice him.

What makes this treatment even worse is that the two parties pictured are at a judicial gathering, a church court assembled to try a dispute between them. The details of differing clothes and standing and sitting can be paralleled in Jewish judicial practice. First Corinthians 6:1-11 mentions that such assemblies, which would have legal authority since at this time the church was viewed as a sect of Judaism and Jewish synagogues, had authority to set up their own courts (*beth-din*) and impose fines or beatings. Certainly in other situations (e.g., worship), posture in church meetings would be uniform (all would sit or stand) and a person's role would be more carefully prescribed. But these two Christians have a dispute, and one thing is clear to the church from the start: the wealthy man must not be offended.

James condemns this behavior on two grounds. First, **you have discriminated among yourselves**. Christ had made them all one: In him there is neither Greek nor Jew, slave nor free, male nor female; but all are one, one new person in Christ (Gal. 3:28). They, however, are conveniently ignoring this fact and distinguishing on the basis of wealth and status in the world, denying the practical effect of Christ's work.

Second, they have **become judges with evil thoughts**. A host of Old Testament passages warns against judicial prejudice, for example: "Do not pervert justice; do not show partiality to

the poor or favoritism to the great, but judge your neighbor fairly"
(Lev. 19:15). If, as the Old Testament claims, God is an impartial
judge and if they claim to judge according to his standards, how
dare they act unjustly, prejudicing their decision in favor of the
rich man because they covet his wealth and power?

While looking at the specific example James gives, however,
one must not ignore the wider application. Would he be any hap-
pier if the poor person were cold-shouldered in a worship meeting? Would the poor person be any less wronged if the preferential
treatment were given the rich in the choice for office in the church?
Or would the discrimination be any less glaring if the pastoral
staff listened carefully to "prime donors" but brushed aside the
suggestions of the poor? As specific as the example is, it functions as a general condemnation of discriminatory behavior.

2:5 / James begins his logical attack on the practice (2:5–
7) with a plea, **Listen, my dear brothers**, calling to their attention
that he is referring to something they already know: **Has not God
chosen those who are poor?** James uses the familiar election terminology of Israel (Deut. 4:37; 7:7) and the church (Eph. 1:4;
1 Pet. 2:9), but he applies it specifically to the poor. Most of the
members of the early church were poor ("few of you were wise
or powerful or of high social standing" [1 Cor. 1:26]), and the Jerusalem church was especially poor (2 Cor. 8:9); but James is saying more than this. God particularly elected **those who are poor
in the eyes of the world** (for it is only with respect to the world's
values that they are poor) **to be rich in faith and to inherit the
kingdom he promised those who love him**. On the one hand,
this makes the poor virtually identical to the one who endures
in 1:12, for both receive what God promised **those who love him**.
On the other hand, James is applying the teaching of Jesus,
for it was Jesus who said he came particularly "to preach good
news [or the gospel] to the poor" (Luke 4:18) and who further
said, "Blessed are you who are poor; for yours is the kingdom
of God" (Luke 6:20). Jesus selected the poor as the special re-
cipients of his kingdom; James picks up this idea adding **those
who love him** to limit the promise to the poor who respond
to the good news. If there are any favorites in God's eyes, they
are the poor, for God has a very different way of viewing them

than the world has. The world sees them as poor, unimportant, but God sees them as **rich (in faith)** and heirs of the Kingdom, a reversal of perspective.

2:6–7 / The church lacks God's perspective: **You have insulted the poor.** God condemns the same crime in the Old Testament (e.g., Prov. 14:21; cf. Sirach 10:22). The church that shames the poor in any way (e.g., 1 Cor. 11:22) has stepped outside of God's will and no longer acts on behalf of God.

The church, however, has shown preference for the rich class, who are its oppressors. First, it is **the rich who are exploiting you.** The idea of the wealthy and powerful exploiting the poor and weak is deeply rooted in the Old Testament (Jer. 7:6; 22:3; Ezek. 18:7; Amos 4:1; 8:4; Mal. 3:5). The poor person needed a loan and the rich gave it to him—for a price (despite the fact that taking interest, i.e., profiting from another's need, was forbidden, e.g., Exod. 22:25–26). If there was a dispute, the rich man hired the best lawyer. They set up society so that the poor got poorer, and the rich richer.

Second, they **are dragging you into court.** When the poor could not repay a loan, the rich dragged them into court to foreclose. Or they may have brought charges of libel against those who complained, or perhaps they even accused the Christians of disturbing the peace and order of the community. In all these ways, Christians experienced some persecution that was simply oppression of all poor by the rich, but sometimes they were singled out because their religion made them especially vulnerable—what judge felt bad about being especially hard on the followers of the despised Galilean?

Third, the rich **are . . . the ones who are slandering the noble name of him to whom you belong.** Now James adds a specifically religious charge. The name of Jesus was given to Christians, or (more literally) called over them at baptism. They now **belong** to him, and he was their Lord. But the rich were speaking evil of this name, either by making fun of Jesus or by insulting his followers. It is not clear whether they were doing this in court as part of their oppression or whether they were insulting Christ in the synagogues and markets. Neither action would have been righteous.

The church, however, had also chosen to insult the poor (whom God honors), and by the same action it had chosen to favor the rich and thus to identify with the oppressing class. It is often the case that an oppressed group takes on the characteristics of its oppressors; when this happens to the church, it is not just pathetically ironic but is a moral reversal, for the people who name the name of Christ are now acting like the people who blaspheme the name of Christ.

2:8–9 / James now proceeds to the biblical argument: **If you really keep the royal** (i.e., of the kingdom) **law . . . you are doing right**. The kingdom in this context (cf. 2:5) is the kingdom of God. While the full glory of this kingdom is still future, the Christian has already entered it and stands under its authority. The law of the kingdom is the Old Testament as interpreted and edited by Jesus, as in Matthew 5–6. To say that one is **doing right** when he or she obeys Jesus' law is a massive understatement: Jesus himself presents his teaching as a matter of life and death (Matt. 7:13–27).

The law is **found in Scripture**, for Jesus generally interpreted the Old Testament rather than speaking without any reference to previous revelation. The specific command that James cites, **Love your neighbor as yourself**, is a favorite of both Jesus (he cites Lev. 19:18 six times in the synoptic Gospels) and the church (Rom. 13:19; Gal. 5:14). It was frequently seen as summing up the law, but James' reason for citing it may be in Proverbs 14:21: "He who despises his neighbor sins, but blessed is he who is kind to the needy (poor)." The poor person is, according to scripture, the neighbor they should love. But these Christians are **show**ing **favoritism**; they are discriminating against the poor, and this is to break this commandment, for it is all connected, as the apocryphal Jewish Testament of Issachar states (in 5:2), "Love the Lord and your neighbor and have compassion on the poor and feeble."

Therefore they **sin**. Their actions are not unfortunate or regrettable or something they should not have done, but simply sin. James is not afraid to use a stark, piercing word to underline the situation, for beating around the bush does not lead to repentance. They **are convicted by the law as lawbreakers**: In this phrase one has a picture of God's last judgment. The person in the dock sees not James, but the personified Law itself, stand up, point its accusing finger, and state, "That person is a transgressor." Such a charge is serious, for Jewish Christians knew that to knowingly transgress the law invited God's judgment upon them.

2:10 / The reason behind this conclusion is a truism: **Whoever keeps the whole law and yet stumbles at just one point is guilty of breaking all of it**. The statement does not mean that it is just as bad no matter which commandment one breaks (e.g., stealing a shoe is as bad as murder) but rather that if one breaks a law one demonstrates an underlying attitude toward the lawgiver and thus is simply a criminal. Deuteronomy 27:26 puts it this way, "Cursed is the [one] who does not uphold the words of this law by carrying them out." The particular offense may have been more or less serious, but the person stands under a curse whichever commandment he or she has broken. James' argument is important in that he is showing that the rebellion against God is more important than the specific act and that no deliberate transgression of God's teachings is unimportant.

2:11 / James illustrates his point using two well-known laws (Exod. 20:13–14; Deut. 5:17–18). **For he**, that is, God, gave both laws. Thus though a Mafia hit man, for example, may pride himself on his marital fidelity while he murders, this does not excuse him in any way before God. He is still simply a **lawbreaker**.

The choice of the two laws may also be significant. Although it is less likely that **adultery** is referring to their adultery with the world (wealth) in 4:4, the reversed order and the fact that in biblical and Jewish tradition murder was often connected to the failure to love one's neighbor or care for the poor may be a sign that their discrimination against the poor brings them under this very charge. **If you do . . . commit murder** may not be entirely hypothetical in James' mind.

2:12 / James' conclusion sums up his biblical argument. In all one's actions one should keep the final judgment in mind. The word pair **speak and act** covers all human behavior (cf. Acts 1:1; 7:22; 1 John 3:18). And both speech and action appear in his example (2:2-4). The command to look at all behavior in the light of judgment fits the situation excellently.

The standard of judgment is **the law gives freedom**, or the law of liberty. The idea has already been mentioned in 1:25, where obedience to this perfect law brings blessing. It is the same as the law of the kingdom of 2:8, namely, the Old Testament as interpreted by Jesus, which will be the standard of judgment (cf. Matt. 7:15-23; Luke 6:43-45). James does not think of this as a forbidding concept, for this law is freeing in that it points away from the bondage of sin and shows the way of life.

2:13 / To back up this argument from scripture (i.e., **because**) and to begin to shift the focus to the next section, James adds a proverbial saying: **judgment without mercy will be shown to anyone who has not been merciful**. God is merciful, as any reader of the Old Testament should know. Exodus 34:5-6 states that when God revealed to Moses his nature and pronounced his name he described himself as "the compassionate and gracious God, slow to anger, abounding in love and faithfulness" (cf. Deut. 4:31; Ps. 103:8-14, which connects this to his judging "in favor of the oppressed"). If this is God's personal standard of righteousness, then it follows that his true followers should copy him. "He has showed you, O man, what is good. And what does the Lord require of you? To act justly and to love mercy and to walk humbly with your God" (Micah 6:8, cf. Hos. 4:1; 6:6; 12:6; Prov. 14:21; Dan. 4:27). Or again, "This is what the Lord Almighty says: 'Administer true justice; show mercy and compassion to one another.'" (Zech. 7:9). Not to show mercy is to step outside of God's covenant and to invite God in return to judge by the same strict standard.

This teaching was made even more explicit in the intertestamental and rabbinic periods. Sirach states, "Does [a person] have no mercy toward a man like himself and yet pray for his own sins?" (Sirach 28:4; cf. 27:30-28:7; Tobit 4:9-11; Testament of Zebulun 8:8), and "Rabbi Barabbi said, 'To him who is merciful to the created, Heaven is merciful, but to him who is unmerciful to the created, Heaven is also unmerciful'" (b. *Shabbath* 151b).

Jesus taught, "Blessed are the merciful, for they will be shown mercy" (Matt. 5:7). This is underlined in his teaching on forgiveness (Matt. 6:14–15), his response to the Pharisees (Matt. 12:7, quoting Hos. 6:6), his parable on forgiveness (Matt. 18:21–35), and his parable of the sheep and the goats (Matt. 25:31–46). Therefore it is the unified witness of the Gospels that Jesus followed standard Jewish teaching and taught that God would show mercy only to those obeying him and doing likewise.

James' use of this saying shows that he had learned Jesus' tradition carefully, for it becomes his clinching argument. Even if the logical and biblical arguments have not convinced the reader that justice and love demand that the poor be treated honorably, then the Christian must still honor the poor person out of mercy and the fear of God's judgment.

Furthermore, **mercy triumphs over judgment!** This is the positive side of the proverb. It is—as the parables of Jesus cited above show—mercy, that is, a person's faithful submission and obedience to God, that conquers judgment. This cuts two ways, for the mercy will destroy both one's judging of others and God's judgment of oneself.

Significant in the choice of words here is the fact that mercy in scripture is not simply charitable evaluation of others but caring for the poor, that is, charity. This not only reflects the previous section of honoring the poor but asks why the Christians were not themselves caring for the poor.

James now focuses on charity and its relevance to faith within the overall topic of the care and appreciation of the poor. The structure is parallel to 2:1–13: in each section James opens with a topic verse, then has an example, a logical argument, and a two-part biblical argument.

2:14 / **My brothers** indicates a new departure in the argument. **What good is it . . . if a man claims to have faith but has no deeds?** The question is purely rhetorical. The form of the question implies James' expectation of a negative answer: No good at all!

The situation is that of saying one has **faith** but lacking **deeds**. In this passage, **faith** has a special meaning for James, that is, orthodox belief conventionally expressed (like "religion" in 1:26). This person can pass the test of orthodoxy, asserting belief in Jesus as Savior. The problem is that his or her lifestyle is identical to that of Jewish (or pagan) neighbors (except for the form of worship): there is no evident self-giving, no detachment from and sharing of wealth. James' response is, **What good is it?**

Again James asks, **Can such faith save him?** The form of this second question also implies the negative answer. There is no salvation for the person who stops short of discipleship. If faith is only intellectual, only expressed in religious practices, it will not save. The Old Testament also condemns piety without action, as do John the Baptist (Luke 3:7–14), Jesus (Matt. 7:15–27), and Paul (Rom. 1:5; 2:6–8; 6:17–18; Gal. 6:4–6). James follows the rest of scripture: faith without actions (discipleship) will never save.

2:15 / James clarifies his point with an example: **Suppose a brother or sister is without clothes and daily food**. James does not pick a hard situation. This is not a case of someone outside the Christian faith (so there can be no "Do you expect us to feed the whole world?" response), nor is this a case of a need in a distant church (like Paul's collection for Jerusalem). This is someone in the community (**a brother or sister**) who clearly has a need, for the person needs **clothes** (either lacking the outer garment that was worn in public places and kept one warm at night or else having clothes in such a ragged condition that they could keep no one warm) and does not have **daily food**. The example, while hypothetical (**suppose**) is both demanding and realistic, for in a marginal society like that in the New Testament it was not unusual for people to lack basic necessities. In fact, in the 40s and 50s famine and starvation conditions hit Judea repeatedly.

2:16 / **If one of you says to him**: This indicates the response of a member of the church: The member of the church who is impoverished has come to another member, and that Christian is turning the brother or sister down.

The words are very pious: **I wish you well** is a standard farewell in the Jewish church; **keep warm and well fed** shows that the material needs of the person have been recognized—the expression is probably a prayer. But if you do **nothing about his physical needs, what good is it?** James assumes that the Christian *could* do more than pray; he or she owns two garments and more than enough food for the day. Simple obedience to the gospel teaching on sharing *could* supply the need, but the resort to prayer salved the conscience and covered up the fact that the cupboard and closet were shut. Such prayers are useless.

2:17 / **In the same way, faith**: The example was a specific example of orthodox language and intellectual belief without gospel obedience. The same is true for intellectual belief in general; if it remains a pious conviction (**by itself**) and fails to result in obedience to the commands of Christ (**not accompanied by action**), it is totally unprofitable (**dead**). For Paul it was only "faith expressing itself through love" that mattered (Gal. 5:6), rather than religious ritual works. For James it is faith that leads to action that saves. Action (obedience to Christ) is no more an "added extra" or a higher optional level of sanctification than breath is an "added extra" to a body (cf. 1:26; 2:14; 2:20; and 2:26).

2:18 / Having given the example, James proceeds to argue his case, employing the lively style of imaginative dialogue, which was as popular with preachers of all types then as it is today.
But someone will say means that just as Paul anticipates an objection in 1 Corinthians 15:35 or Romans 9:19 so James anticipates one here. The objection is: **You have faith; I have deeds**, in other words, the claim that faith and action are different gifts. Did not Paul write about varieties of gifts but the same Spirit (1 Cor. 12:4–10)? Faith is a gift and so is charity (Rom. 12:8). Is there any reason for one to suspect that faith and action would come together in the same person any more than healing and tongues or prophecy and evangelism?
James answers with a demand that is common to this kind of speech: **Show me** [or "prove to me"] **your faith without deeds**. A better translation would be "Prove your faith without action." This demand is impossible to meet. Like a horse that cannot be seen, smelled, touched, or ridden, that eats invisible grass and leaves no mark on the ground, such faith is indemonstrable and suspect. Faith is seen in lifestyle, or as Paul states in 1 Corinthians 13:2, "If I had all . . . faith but had not love, I am nothing."
On the other hand, **I will show you my faith by what I do**. Though a claim to faith without resultant life is suspect, so conversely Christian action demands one posit a motivation be-

hind it. No one lives like Jesus *without faith in Jesus.* The sermon
preached by a life of action does not need to buttonhole people
to get a hearing; instead, people hearing the unwritten sermon
of action *request* an explanation in terms of the faith that motivates it.

2:19 / James has not yet put to rest the specter of dead
orthodoxy, so he turns to the assertion of belief itself and accepts
it at face value. **You believe that there is one God. Good!** This
is the most basic teaching of Judaism and Christianity, being the
first part of the Shema. This confession of faith was recited two
times a day by every Pharisaic Jew, "Hear, O Israel: The Lord our
God, the Lord is one. Love the Lord your God with all your heart
and with all your soul and with all your strength" (Deut. 6:4–5;
the fullest form of the Shema included Deut. 6:4–9; 11:13–21;
Num. 15:37–41). Such a confession of faith was a starting place
for Christians as well, for Jesus had referred to it as the greatest
commandment (Mark 12:28–34). Paul would assert "there is only
one God" (Rom. 3:30). Hermas would later write that the most
basic tenet of Christianity is "First of all, believe that God is one"
(*Mandate* 1). So although Christians believe more than this, this
belief is the starting point.

But James' praise is partly tongue-in-cheek: **Even the
demons believe that—and shudder.** The orthodoxy of the demons
was well known not only in Judaism but also in the New Testament, where the demons frequently give fuller confessions of
Christ than the apostles (Mark 1:24; 5:7; Acts 16:17; 19:15). Their
problem is that their response to the name of God (the reminder
of their orthodox knowledge) is to **shudder**, because they are in
rebellion against that God. All their orthodox knowledge simply
makes them tremble, for their "faith" does not lead to obedient
action. Likewise, those who can only claim an orthodox confession of faith are doing no better than Satan if they have not committed themselves to lives of obedience.

2:20 / James has completed his theological argument but
will add concrete scriptural illustrations. Before citing these passages he adds (as was common in the homiletic style of the day):
You foolish man. The address seems strong—hardly polite—and

it is, as the term **fool** indicates, not primarily an intellectual error, but a moral error. Yet the strong language was normal for that day: One need only cite Jesus (Matt. 23:17; Luke 24:25) or Paul (1 Cor. 15:36; Gal. 3:1) to be able to guess accurately that Jewish teachers of all types and Greek teachers as well used similar language.

The content of the appeal is almost equally strong: **Do you want evidence that faith without deeds is useless?** This suggests that it is the person's willful ignorance that is demanding more proof and may make it impossible to accept the proof. A searching mind receives evidence quickly, but the willfully ignorant can never be shown enough evidence. Yet James makes the charitable assumption and continues the discussion.

2:21 / The first character discussed is **our ancestor Abraham**. A gentile Christian could have written this expression, thinking of the church as the New Israel (Rom. 4; Gal. 2:7, 29), but it is more likely the unconscious reference of a Jewish Christian. Yet, in a sense, Abraham *is* the father of all the faithful, and the reference fits all Christians.

Abraham was **considered righteous**. With this translation the NIV correctly differentiates James' terminology from that of Paul. James uses the standard meaning of this term, "declared right by God" or "considered righteous by God", whereas Paul uses the same language in a unique way ("make [a sinner] right"). James' meaning clearly flows from the Old Testament passage which lies behind his conclusion, Genesis 22:12, in which God says, "Now I know that you fear God," the "now I know" being the declaration of righteousness. (This difference in meaning, of course, is another indication that James had not had contact with Paul's work.)

The basis of the declaration was actions: It was **for what he did when he offered his son Isaac on the altar**. Abraham's faith in God was real because it governed Abraham's life. The word **what he did** is plural, because in selecting the offering of Isaac James points to the Jewish tradition in which this was the capstone of all Abraham's actions. "Was not Abraham found faithful when tested, and it was reckoned to him as righteousness?" (1 Macc. 2:52). The tests referred to are a series of ten tests, cul-

minating in the sacrifice of Isaac, which were Abraham's works
of charity: "Abraham woke up charity which slept. For he opened
an inn, and received within it the passersby" (*Midrash on Psalms*
on Ps. 110:1). The basis of his legendary charity was Genesis 18
as interpreted by tradition. Thus Genesis 15:6 was seen as an anticipatory declaration in the light of subsequent action revealing
true faith. The declaration of righteousness comes in two ways:
First is the fact that God inexplicably aborts the sacrifice, as this
later Jewish story illustrates:

> The angels then broke into loud weeping, and they exclaimed:
> "The highways lie waste, the wayfaring man ceaseth, he [God]
> hath broken the covenant. Where is the regard of Abraham, he
> who took the wayfarers into his house, gave them food and drink,
> and went with them to bring them on their way? . . . for the
> slaughtering knife is set upon his throat." [Then God in response
> acknowledges Abraham's righteousness by ordering him to stop.]

Second is the "now I know" statement of Genesis 22:12; Abraham had a lived-out faith that had resulted in righteous actions
that in turn were declared right by God.

2:22 / James continues: **You see.** Surely the point of the
passages cited was clear; **His faith and his actions were working
together.** (Or, "his faith worked with his actions.") But where did
the faith come from? The answer lies in the Jewish traditions about
Abraham. These asserted that Abraham, who lived in an idola-
trous culture, had contemplated nature, and this had led him to
the one God. He had rejected idolatry, burned the local house
of gods, and committed himself to the one God (the story is nar-
rated in the apocryphal book of Jubilees 11–12). Thus Abraham
was the originator of the creed "there is one God" (James 2:19).

Given this background, it is clear that a Jewish Christian
would understand how faith and actions worked together. Unlike Terah in the legends, who agrees with Abraham's faith but
through fear of the people tells Abraham to keep quiet and hold
this faith in his heart, Abraham acts consistently with his faith.
His faith works with or directs his actions.

Furthermore, **his faith was made complete by what he did.**
The idea is not that faith was perfected in the sense of it having
been less than faith before, but that faith is brought to maturity

through action (cf. 1:4, 15). There is a mutuality: Faith informs and motivates action; action matures faith. James is not rejecting one for the other but is instead insisting that the two are totally inseparable.

2:23 / James draws two conclusions. First, **and the scripture was fulfilled that says, "Abraham believed God, and it was credited to him as righteousness."** Although Paul also cites this passage (Rom. 4:3; Gal. 3:6), he and James interpret it differently. For Paul the point is that Abraham believed God and was declared righteous *before* he was circumcised and thus before keeping the ritual law. James (like 1 Macc. 2:52) sees the two parts of the sentence as separate statements. The first is **Abraham believed God**, or "had faith in God." That was true; all Jewish tradition witnessed to his belief that God is one. The second is **it was credited to him as righteousness**, or better, "God declared him righteous." This was also true. Abraham expressed his faith at every turn, whether in welcoming strangers (charity), refusing reward from the king of Sodom, or offering his son Isaac. Thus both parts of the sentence are true, and the scripture in Genesis makes the same point about Abraham as James has been arguing.

The second conclusion is **and he was called God's friend**. Unlike the first conclusion, this is not a direct biblical quotation but a rough paraphrase of the sense of Isaiah 41:8 or 2 Chronicles 20:7. Its significance is that the Jews connected the title "friend" with Abraham's faithfulness and obedience under testing. Thus the apocryphal Jewish work Jubilees, after recounting the completion of the tenth test of Abraham, concludes, "he was found faithful, and was recorded on the heavenly tablets as the friend of God" (19:9). In harmony with this idea, James points out that the fact that God refers to Abraham as a friend also shows that he had more than an intellectual faith; he had an active faithfulness expressed in obedience.

2:24 / James summarizes: **You see that a person is justified by what he does and not by faith alone.** This summary, which is addressed to the "my brothers" of 2:14, not the objector of 2:18, causes a problem, for it appears that James is contradicting Paul, who writes in Romans 3:28, "For we maintain that a man is justified by faith apart from observing the law" (cf. Rom. 3:20; 4:16). This problem can be resolved by careful interpretation.

First, **by what he does** means for James works of love and charity (as in 1:27), whereas Paul is always concerned about "observing the law," meaning specifically the ritual law, for example, circumcision, dietary regulations, sacrifices. Paul expected every Christian to do works of love and charity (e.g., Eph. 2:10; Gal. 6:9–10) and also believed that those who failed to follow through in this area were not among the "saved" (e.g., Gal. 5:19–21; 1 Cor. 6:9–10; Rom. 1:28–32).

Second, **a person is justified** is a poor translation (unlike that in 2:21 above), for it reads the Pauline meaning of this term (the forgiveness which repentant sinners receive at God's judgment seat when they put their trust in Christ) into James. James is still using the older and more standard meaning of the term, "a person is declared to be righteous by God" or "is considered righteous by God" and this "on the basis on what he does" (and not on the basis of what ideas he agrees to).

Third, **not by faith alone** means for James "by intellectual belief that God is one" or "that Jesus is Lord," whereas faith for Paul means personal commitment to Christ that leads inevitably to obedience because one is convinced that Jesus is Lord. For Paul the concern is to prove that one is not "saved" by ritual actions ("observing the law," or the "works of the law"). He would never consider separating faith and actions the way James does, except to refute such a separation (e.g., Rom. 6–8). Therefore, though Paul uses "alone" with ritual works (Rom. 4:16), James uses it with faith to show its illegitimate total separation from action.

James' point is that God will not approve a person just because he or she is very orthodox or can pass a test in systematic theology. He will declare someone righteous only if this faith is such that the person acts on it and produces the natural result of commitment, obedient action. With such a point Paul would not disagree.

2:25 / James continues, introducing a second illustration, **Rahab the prostitute**, whose words and actions in Joshua 2:1–21 fascinated the Jews as well as the early Christians (Heb. 11:31). Again the translation **considered righteous** is the correct one.

Again there is a faith-action combination. Rahab had faith, for in Joshua 2:9–10 she confesses a faith that came from reflection on what God had done for Israel. But her faith was not enough to deliver her; she had to act by giving **lodging to the spies** and then sending **them off in a different direction**, which meant risking her life. Hebrews 11:31 similarly stresses faith-motivated action: "By faith the prostitute Rahab, because she welcomed the spies, was not killed with those who were disobedient." Faith alone would not have saved her, but when faith led to action the spies declared her righteous. She became one of the promised people and an ancestor of David (and Jesus) because her faith was that of committed action, not intellectual reflection.

2:26 / With **so**, James welds together the themes of 2:14 and 2:17 to form a concluding verse: **As the body without the spirit is dead, so faith without deeds is dead.** A body without spirit (or breath) is a corpse. Jews were aware that it was when a person "breathed his last" or "gave up his spirit" (the words for breath and spirit being identical in both Greek and Hebrew) he was dead (John 19:30; Luke 23:46; Ecclesiastes 3:21; 8:8; 9:5). A dead body is a liability that must be buried. Likewise faith that remains intellectual belief is dead. It cannot save; it is a liability, for it can deceive a person as to his or her true spiritual state. Only when faith becomes full commitment and is joined to actions does it have value.

Additional Notes §2

2:1 / The term for partiality (*prosōpolēmpsia*) was coined by the Christian ethical tradition on the basis of the Old Testament statements about God and applied especially to God's judgment (Acts 10:34; Rom. 2:11; Eph. 6:9; Col. 3:25; 1 Pet. 1:17). See further E. Lohse, "*Prosōpolēmpsia*," *TDNT*, vol. 6, pp. 779–80.

The phrase **our glorious Lord Jesus Christ** is awkward Greek. S. S. Laws, *James*, pp. 95–97; and J. B. Mayor, *James*, pp. 80–82, argue for a titular use parallel to John 14:6, "our Lord Jesus Christ, the Glory." Some ancient translations believe the faith is what is glorious, i.e., "the glorious faith of our Lord Jesus Christ." The translation that this commentary prefers, on the analogy of Eph. 6:24 and James 1:25, is that of the NIV **our glorious Lord Jesus Christ** (see further M. Dibelius, *James*, p. 128; J. H. Ropes, *James* p. 187). If this is the correct interpretation then Christ is seen as the expression of God's own glory, which surrounded his presence in the Old Testament, particularly when he acted to save Israel. In the New Testament this reference is especially applied to God's coming salvation of his people, i.e., his eschatological deliverance (Matt. 16:27; 24:30; John 1:14; 17:5; Rom. 8:17; 1 Cor. 2:8; Titus 2:13; 1 Pet. 4:13). By using this term James removes his readers' focus from their present situation and reminds them that the present world is transitory. See further S. Aalen, "Glory, Honor," *NIDNTT*, vol. 2, pp. 44–48.

On Jesus and the Bible's attitude toward wealth see further R. Sider, *Cry Justice* (Downers Grove, Ill.: Inter-Varsity Press, 1980), pp. 124–46.

2:2 / The **rich man** in the example is never called rich in the Greek text. He is simply referred to as a person with **a gold ring and fine clothes**, from which his wealth is correctly inferred. James never uses the Greek word for rich (*plousios*) when writing about wealthy Christians (cf. 4:13–17) but does when referring to pagans (1:10–11; 2:6; 5:1–6). The rich are by definition outside the kingdom (cf. Luke 6:24). The other person, however, is expressly called **poor** (*ptōchos*), for that is almost a title for the Christian community (cf. 2:5).

The person enters **your meeting**; James uses *synagōgē* instead of the usual term for church, *ekklēsia* (5:14). *Synagōgē* occasionally refers to Christian gatherings until the time of Ignatius and Hermas (*Mandate* 11.9, 13–14) as W. Schrage, "*Synagōgē*," *TDNT*, vol. 7, pp. 840–41 shows, but it is unusual, being chosen because James is not referring to an assembly for worship but to a special assembly. The word itself means a gathering.

It is in Jewish sources that one reads of the importance of similar clothing and posture in judicial assemblies (e.g., *Deut. Rabba* 5:6 on Deut. 16:19; b. *Shebuot* 30a; 31a; t. *Sanhedrin* 6:2; *Aboth de R. Nathan* 1:10; *Sipra Kedoshim* 4:4 on Lev. 19:15). For further data see R. B. Ward, "Partiality in the Assembly."

2:4 / **Have you not discriminated . . . ?** is in some translations phrased as a statement rather than a question. The Greek text does have a question, but the form of the question makes it clear that he is not really expressing doubt but making his charge in interrogative form.

Become judges with evil thoughts can be translated "evilly motivated judges" like the "unjust judge" of Luke 18:6. Cf. the Jewish condemnation of such behavior: e.g., Prov. 18:5; Psalms of Solomon 2:18; b. *Berakoth* 6a.

2:5 / God's election of Israel is further discussed by L. Coenen, "Elect," *NIDNTT*, vol. 1, pp. 539–42.

God's interest in the poor was not only a major part of the Old Testament tradition (e.g., Deut. 15; Prov. 19:17; Ps. 35:10) but also very much a part of the intertestamental period; e.g., 1 Enoch 108:7–15; Psalms of Solomon 5; *Gen. Rabba* 71:1. See further E. Bammel, *"Ptōchos," TDNT,* vol. 6, pp. 895–98; R. Sider, *Rich Christians in an Age of Hunger* (Downers Grove, Ill: Inter-Varsity Press, 1977), pp. 59–86; R. Foster, *The Freedom of Simplicity* (San Francisco: Harper & Row, 1981), pp. 15–51.

The promise of the **kingdom** of God to the poor is found throughout the New Testament, e.g., Matt. 5:3, where "poor in spirit" should be interpreted as those poor who have the proper spirit of dependence on God; it cannot be expanded to include people who have no real needs in life. The kingdom is further discussed in Matt. 25:34; 1 Cor. 6:9–10; Gal. 5:21. In all these cases the kingdom is equivalent to salvation. See further G. E. Ladd, *A Theology of the New Testament* (Grand Rapids: Eerdmans, 1974), pp. 57–69.

2:6 / In making his charges against the rich, James again uses rhetorical questions expecting a positive answer, which the NIV has correctly restructured into question-and-answer form.

Note the shift of number that happens in this verse. They dishonor **the poor** person (singular). This person is one of their own group, an individual. But **the rich** are a class (plural), a group outside the church. At this point the author shifts to the word "rich" (*plousios,* cf. 2:2), for he is not referring to a wealthy individual in the church but to an oppressing class that the church *as a group* is imitating.

When the Old Testament speaks of "oppression," e.g., Ezek. 22:7, 29; Heb. 1:4; Zech. 7:10, it rarely calls the oppressor "the rich" but normally uses the term "the violent." However, it is clear that the oppressors are invariably wealthy and powerful. Thus it is not surprising to see a shift in later Judaism and the New Testament to identify the term "rich" with oppression. See further E. Bammel, *"Ptōchos," TDNT,* vol. 6, p. 888.

The idea of dragging one before the judges is not a use of the usual term for arresting a person. It indicated injustice or persecution, as in Acts 16:19; 21:20.

2:8 / Some see the **royal law** as a Jewish reference to the kingship of Yahweh. Others, e.g., Dibelius, *James,* p. 143, view it as a law having sovereign authority, citing 4 Macc. 14:2 as a parallel. Still others believe this epithet **royal** refers to its rank among other commands (cf. Matt. 12:31). Probably the reference is to its being a law of the kingdom of which Jesus is king, first, because that sense of kingdom appears in 2:5; second, because James uses the term "law" (which normally refers to a body of law), not commandment (which refers to a single law); and third, because this sense of **royal** most underlines the seriousness of their action. See further, V. P. Furnish, *The Love Command in the New Testament* (Nashville: Abingdon, 1972), pp. 179–80.

2:9 / On the connection between love and caring for the poor see also G. F. Moore, *Judaism in the First Centuries of the Christian Era* (Cambridge, Mass.: Harvard University Press, 1927), vol. 2, pp. 84–88.

The term **sin** is found frequently in James, e.g., 4:17; 5:16, 17, 20. His goal (5:20) is to turn sinners from the error of their ways. Jesus also spoke about doing sin (Matt. 7:23).

The idea of being a transgressor or **lawbreaker** is found in Rom. 2:25, 27; Gal. 2:8 and also in the Talmud, e.g., *b. Shabbath* 11a. See further S. Schechter, *Some Aspects of Rabbinic Theology.*

2:10 / The idea of the unity of the law is found in such Jewish writings as 4 Macc. 5:20 and Testament of Asher 2:5, as well as rabbinic writings. It also occurs elsewhere in the New Testament, e.g., Matt. 5:18–19, with its emphasis on the least commandment, or Gal. 5:3, where Paul insists that one cannot take the law piecemeal.

2:11 / The reversed order of the commands in the Decalogue does appear in a few Hebrew and Greek texts of the Old Testament as well as in Luke 18:20 and Rom. 13:9, so one cannot be sure that James' order is deliberate. Yet Jer. 7:6; 22:3; Amos 8:4; Sirach 34:26; Testament of Gad 4:6–7, and 1 John 3:15 all associate murder with the failure to care for the poor. Thus there was a strong Jewish and Christian tradition for James to use. James is conceptually so close to 1 John that this parallel passage may be very significant.

2:12 / James speaks frequently of judgment, e.g., 1:19; 3:1–12; 4:11–16, and 5:12 speak of words being judged, and 1:27; 4:1–10; 5:1–6 speak of deeds. But Jesus also gave solemn warnings in Matt. 12:36; 25:31–45.

J. B. Adamson, *James*, pp. 118–19, contrasts the law of liberty of 2:12 with the law of ordinances in 2:10–11, seeing a law–grace dichotomy consonant with his reformed theology. But there is no evidence in the text that this was in *James'* mind. He feels perfectly comfortable with enjoying grace within a structure of ethical rules.

2:13 / Judgment without mercy is not injustice but rather strict justice without forgiveness. See further E. E. Urbach, *The Sages.*

Mercy **triumphs** over judgment in the sense of "boast in triumphant comparison with other," as R. Bultmann points out ("*Katakauchaomai*," *TDNT*, vol. 3, pp. 653–54). In comparison with the strictness of judgment, mercy is more powerful.

The sense of mercy meaning charity is already evident in the Old Testament passages cited. For example, the wider context of Zech. 7:9 explicitly mentions caring for the poor as the focus of mercy. In the New Testament the Greek for mercy, *eleos*, or merciful, *eleēmones* (Matt. 5:7), is closely related to giving alms or charity, *eleēmosynē* (Matt. 6:2). New Testament mercy is not reactive, simply not giving someone what he or she deserves, but proactive, i.e., meeting the needs of another whether or not that person has a formal claim on the giver (Luke 10:37, the good Samaritan). Furthermore, mercy is pre-eminently an attribute of **God** and thus a characteristic taken on by those being transformed into God's likeness in Christ.

2:14 / The **what good is it** form also appears in 1 Cor. 15:32. The second rhetorical question (**Can such faith save him?**) begins with the Greek negative *mē*, which introduces questions expecting a negative answer.

That **save** refers to salvation in the final judgment is seen when one considers the judgment already spoken of in 2:13; the references to such salvation in 1:21; 4:12; 5:20 and the general meaning of **save** in the New Testament. See further W. Foerster, "*Sōzō*," *TDNT*, vol. 7, pp. 990–98.

For the prophetic denunciation of piety without works, see e.g., Amos 5:21–24; Micah 4:1–4, and J. Miranda, *Marx and the Bible*, pp. 111–60. Paul is in full agreement: The works Paul is against are the "works of the law," the ritual actions of the law, like circumcision, used to gain salvation. When it comes to evil (e.g., Gal. 5:19–21), he can say that those doing certain things "will not possess the kingdom of God." On the other hand, he points out that the whole purpose of salvation is good works (Eph. 2:10). Jews had a similar faith-works position. See m. *Aboth* 1:2 or S. Schechter, *Some Aspects of Rabbinic Theology*, p. 214, or G. F. Moore, *Judaism in the First Centuries of the Christian Era* (Cambridge, Mass.: Harvard University Press, 1927), vol. 2, pp. 168–69.

2:15 / The **without clothes** in Greek is literally "naked." This means, however, the lacking of an outer garment (Job 22:6; 24:7; 31:9; Isa. 20:5; 58:7; Matt. 25:36; John 21:7; 2 Cor. 11:27). Rabbi Akiba and his wife had only one outer garment between them, so one stayed home while the other wore the garment to the market or the rabbinic school. At night they buried themselves in straw to keep warm.

The **without . . . daily food** in Greek is not the same as Matt. 6:11 but means the same. James has used a form more common in classical Greek.

2:16 / **Go, I wish you well** is the common Hebrew dismissal, which was actually blessing the person (Judg. 18:6; 1 Sam. 1:17; 20:42; Mark 5:34; Acts 16:36). The wish for peace (Hebrew *shalôm*, which means health or wholeness) was taken so seriously that 2 John 10–11 prohibits Christians from giving such greetings to false teachers.

The **physical needs** are the food and clothing the person cannot survive without. Any Jew or Jewish Christian would have understood the imperative of charity in such a case, for as R. Hiyya said: "He who turns his eyes away from almsgiving is as if he worshipped idols" (b. *Kettubim* 68a, from C. G. Montefiore and H. Loewe, *A Rabbinic Anthology* [New York: Schocken Books, 1974], p. 413; see further pp. 412–39). Jesus' parable of the rich man and Lazarus (Luke 16:19–31) taught that the failure to meet an obvious need despite having the means damns a person.

2:17 / The term **by itself** is particularly close to the body-breath analogy and might have suggested it to James (2:26).

2:18 / Although the general meaning of the passage is clear, the language is so difficult some scholars have assumed that part of this verse has disappeared. Two other positions have merit. One argues that the voice is favorable to James and restates his position of 2:17: "You (claim to) have faith, and I (you admit) have works. Show me your 'faith' apart from your works (you cannot, naturally), and I will show you my faith by means of my works" (see further J. B. Mayor, *James*, pp. 124–25, 135–37). In that case the voice merges back into James' voice in v. 20 or 21. Grammatically this is possible, but the stumbling block is the fact that in other places in Greek literature the **someone will say** introduction always introduces a hostile or opposing voice (see also Luke 4:23; Rom. 11:9; 4 Macc. 2:24; Barnabas 9:6; Josephus, *Wars* 8.363). A second position, followed in the NIV and this commentary, argues that this sentence is an objection and that although "you" and "I" are used in the Greek they are simply a distributive "one . . . another." Thus the "you" and "I" refer to no one in particular but indicate two different individuals. (M. Dibelius, *James*, p. 156, cites a similar example in Teles.) Though this explanation is grammatically awkward, it is consonant with the introductory phrase and does not resort to emendation. See further J. H. Ropes, *James*, pp. 208–14; C. L. Mitton, *James*, pp. 108–9; S. S. Laws, *James*, pp. 123–24.

2:19 / The fact that James writes **you believe that** rather than "you believe in" shows that he is thinking of intellectual belief rather than personal commitment. See further R. Bultmann, "*Pisteuō*," *TDNT*, vol. 6, pp. 210–12.

The form of the Shema in this verse is translated in the NIV "there is one God," following one set of Greek manuscripts. However, the reading "God is one," found in other manuscripts, is probably the one James actually wrote. Though the Shema was the beginning point for Christians in a pagan world (e.g., 1 Thess. 1:9), it was not the end point of faith. For the Jew as well, the Shema was not the end, for it led to keeping the law as an expression of faith. The fact that James cites the Shema may also be connected to his citation of Abraham in 2:21, for Abraham was believed in Judaism to have discovered and taught this truth that God is one, despite his pagan environment and persecution. See further R. N. Longenecker, *Paul, Apostle of Liberty* (Grand Rapids: Baker Book House, 1976), pp. 79–83.

That the demons **shudder** or tremble was also known outside Christianity. For example, in the apocryphal work 1 Enoch, when Enoch sees the fallen angels, he states, "Then I spoke to them all together, and they were all afraid, and fear and trembling seized them" (1 Enoch 13:3; cf. 69:1, 14). One reason for the trembling was that the name of God was invoked in exorcisms. See further A. Deissmann, *Light from the Ancient East* (Grand Rapids: Baker Book House, 1927, 1978), especially p. 260; and J. Jeremias, "Paul and James," *ExpTim* 66 (1955), p. 370.

2:20 / The term for **you foolish man** (used differently in 4:5) is the Greek equivalent for *raca* of Matt. 5:22 ("you fool," NIV; RSV; "you good-for-nothing," GNB). In the Septuagint *kenos* is used in Judg. 9:4; 11:3, meaning moral error rather than intellectual lack. Similar strong language occurs in the Stoic Epictetus and the Christian Hermas: "And she cried out with a loud voice and said, 'Oh, foolish man! Do you not see the tower is still being built?' " (*Vision* 3.8.9). See further A. Oepke, "*Kenos*," *TDNT*, vol. 3, p. 659.

The term **useless** in **faith without deeds is useless** is not the same word used in 2:17, 26 or 1:26. It is a term meaning "sterile," "unproductive," "useless" (Matt. 12:36; 20:3, 6; 1 Tim. 5:13; Titus 1:13; 2 Pet. 1:8), forming (in Greek) a wordplay with **actions**.

2:21 / **Our ancestor Abraham** was sometimes used by the Gentiles; 1 Clement 31:2 asks, "Why was our forefather Abraham blest? Was it not because he acted in righteousness and dependability through faith?" but Jews referred to him far more frequently this way, e.g., Isa. 51:2; 4 Macc. 16:20; Matt. 3:9; John 8:39; m. *Aboth* 5:2).

The tests of Abraham are referred to in a variety of late Jewish literature, e.g., *Aboth de. R. Nathan* 32; m. *Aboth* 5:3; Jubilees 17:17; 19:8; *Pirke R. Eliezer* 26–31, as is his great charity: Testament of Abraham, recension A, 1.17; Targum Ps.–Jonathan on Gen. 21:33; *Aboth de R. Nathan* 7. Translation of the last-named as well as of the *Midrash on Psalms* passage cited in the text can be found in C. G. Montefiore and H. Loewe, *A Rabbinic Anthology*, pp. 415 and 564 respectively. See further L. Ginzberg, *Legends of the Jews*, vol. 1, p. 281. Further passages are cited in R. B. Ward, "The Works of Abraham: James 2:14–26," pp. 286–90; and P. H. Davids, "Tradition and Interpretation in the Epistle of James," pp. 113–16.

On the concept of declaring right at the end of a test see further B. Gerhardsson, *The Testing of God's Son*, esp. p. 27.

2:22 / Gen. 15:6 (cf. James 2:23) speaks of **faith**, but that does not explain the particular emphasis James gives to it. Furthermore, although only the Jubilees version was cited, there are multiple versions of the Abraham legend. In the midrash *Genesis Rabba* 98:3, for example, the Shema is traced back to Abraham. Josephus has his version in *Antiquities* 1.154–157 (1.7.1 in Whiston's division): "[Abraham] was the first that ventured to publish this notion that there was but one God, the Creator of the universe." Philo also refers to the legend (*Legum Allegoriae* 3.228; *De Virtue* 216). Thus all Jews in the New Testament period thought of Abraham as the first to discover monotheistic faith.

2:23 / The form of argument is a typical Jewish exegesis or midrash, with a first text (the Abraham history) having already been discussed and now secondary texts being added. **The scripture was fulfilled** is not in the sense of prediction fulfillment, but in the sense of the scripture agreeing with the scriptural narrative. See further R. N. Longenecker, *Biblical Exegesis in the Apostolic Period*, pp. 32–38.

The Jews frequently referred to the Gen. 15:6 passage, **Abraham believed God.** Not only 1 Macc. 2:52 uses it but also Jubilees 15:6; Philo

(*De Abrahamo* 262; *Quod Deus sit Immutabilis* 4); and several passages in early rabbinic midrash. James' use follows this moderate tradition, not that, for example, of the Targum Ps.-Jonathan (on Gen. 15:6), where the faith of Abraham is itself seen as a work.

It was credited to him as righteousness is passive in the Greek Old Testament ("it was reckoned to him for righteousness") but active in Hebrew ("he accounted it to him [as?] righteousness"). James apparently understands this active sense and thus sees Abraham's faith as one part of the sentence, and "he accounted him righteous" as the second part. The idea of accounting was understood in James' day as entering in the heavenly books. See further H. W. Heidland, "*Logizomai,*" *TDNT,* vol. 4, pp. 284–92.

That Abraham was counted God's friend and that this was connected to his deeds is clear from Jubilees 30:20; 2 Esdras 3:14; and 1 Clement 10:1 (who shares James' tradition), as well as the passage cited. See further J. Jeremias, "*Abraam,*" *TDNT,* vol. 1, pp. 8–9.

2:24 / The **you see** is a shift from second person singular (the "you" of 2:18, 19, 20, 22) to second person plural.

The supposed James-Paul conflict is a major issue. J. T. Sanders, *Ethics in the New Testament,* pp. 115–28, sets James against Paul in such a way as to force the reader to reject one or the other. Luther, for whom the problem was also acute, opted for Paul and almost rejected James from the canon. Luther was correct that if James knew and understood Paul's doctrine so that he used his words with the same meanings, then James is directly contradicting Paul. What Luther failed to understand was that he was reading Paul's meaning backwards into James. James uses words so differently from Paul that if he had ever heard Paul's teaching (as he might not have before A.D. 49), he had only heard it in the form of second- or third-hand slogans, which had taken on a meaning that Paul would have rejected.

The three critical terms discussed illustrate this point. The first is the Greek *ergon,* which in James means **what he does** (charity, kindness, virtue), whereas in Paul it is always joined to the word "law" (*nomos*) and always means ritual acts, *except* in Gal. 5:19 and 6:4 where it is used *positively.* The second is *dikaioō,* which is translated in Paul correctly as "put right with God," whereas James uses it as it is used forty-four times in the Septuagint for "declared to be right by God." Where Paul's new meaning is read into James, total misunderstanding results. Finally there is the word **faith** (*pistis*), which James uses in three ways himself, for true commitment (2:5), for Christianity (2:1), and for intellectual belief (2:14–26). He only has problems with this last type of "faith" and then only if unconnected to works (**faith alone**). Paul normally uses it in one of the two first meanings, which include the actions about which James is so adamant.

James' teaching, then, is that of Matt. 7:15–21, that all one's orthodox assertions will not substitute for obedience as a proof of heart commitment when it comes to the final judgment. Paul believed the same (1 Cor. 13:2; 2 Cor. 9:8; Gal. 5:6; 6.4; Eph. 4:17ff.; Col. 3:5ff.), but James is closer in phrasing and life-setting to his master Jesus.

See further J. Jeremias, "Paul and James," *ExpTim* 66 (1955–1956); J. A. Ziesler, *The Meaning of Righteousness in Paul* (Cambridge: Cambridge Univ. Press, 1972), pp. 9–14; E. L. Allen, "Controversy in the New Testament," *NTS* 1 (1954–1955), pp. 143–49; and especially H. C. Hahn. "Work," *NIDNTT*, vol. 3, pp. 1147–52; H. Seebass and C. Brown, "Righteousness," *NIDNTT*, vol. 3, pp. 352–77; O. Michel, "Faith," *NIDNTT*, vol. 1, pp. 393–607.

2:25 / **Rahab** was viewed by Jesus as the archetypal proselyte to Judaism, and traditions about her abounded. In Christian literature, not only Heb. 11:31 (which stresses her action) praises her, but also 1 Clement 12:1, 8, which is part of a larger section, 1 Clement 9–12. In this section, after a brief mention of Enoch and Noah, Abraham is treated thoroughly as one "called the friend, proved faithful in that he obeyed the words of God." Especially "his faith and hospitality" are named. Lot, who comes next, is cited for "hospitality and piety." Then Clement continues, "Because of her faith and hospitality Rahab the harlot was saved." Thus in the early church Rahab was grouped with Abraham, perhaps because both turned from their respective pagan environments to serve God. It is no coincidence that James cites both in order. Furthermore, both are cited as examples of faith and charity, for in the East hospitality was an important form of charity (e.g., Heb. 13:2). See further H. Chadwick, "Justification by Faith and Hospitality," *SP* 4 (1961), p. 281.

2:26 / In Gen. 2:7 the first human is formed of **spirit**, or breath, and **body**. The union of the two produces a living being, whether in creation or in the womb (Eccles. 11:5). When one dies, the spirit or breath returns to God and the body crumbles into dust (Eccles. 12:7). Spirit and breath are identical words in Hebrew and in Greek (*rûaḥ* and *pneuma* respectively), so breathing one's last is often seen as giving up spirit (e.g., Gen. 49:33; cf. John 19:30; Luke 23:46; and Mark 15:37 for three descriptions of the same death). For the Jew and Christian death is never welcome. Their Greek neighbors rejoiced in the freeing of the immortal soul from the prison of the body. The Christian, by way of contrast, did not want to be unclothed (without a body), but clothed with a resurrected body (2 Cor. 5:1–10; cf. 1 Cor. 15); the redemption of the body was the real hope (Rom. 8:23). James follows normal Christian practice in seeing a corpse as useless and bad.

§3 Wisdom for the Tongue (James 3:1–18)

Like the Pauline churches, James' church was a church of the Spirit. Though there were formal offices, such as elder (5:14), there was no ordination process or schooling needed to teach and preach. As a result it was relatively easy for people with some ability, but worldly motivation, to put themselves forward as teachers. (Our modern seminary-ordination process makes this take longer, but it is not successful in preventing it; rather, it makes such a person a more permanent fixture in the church.) These uncalled teachers criticized others and formed cliques in the church; other church members followed suit in speaking harshly of them. James' response is to call for control of the tongue, citing the danger of the tongue, giving the marks of God's Spirit, and finally exposing the worldly motivation of many in the church.

3:1 / My brothers indicates the beginning of a section. **Not many of you should presume to be teachers**: Teachers were important for the church (Rom. 12:7; 1 Cor. 12:28; Eph. 4:11–13), but the church was also plagued by false teachers (e.g., 1 Tim. 1:7; Titus 1:11; 2 Pet. 2:1). The gift of teaching was easy to counterfeit, if someone were eloquent enough. But as surely as a person had "volunteered" to teach rather than having been impelled by the Spirit, so surely would his or her worldly motives become manifest in jealously, strife, or heresy. James values the ministry, but he realizes that its social attractiveness and power make it dangerous and that one should be reluctant to enter it.

The danger of the ministry is first of all personal: **We who teach will be judged more strictly**. If every casual word would be judged, how much more the words of those who dealt in words? (Matt. 12:36). If the Jewish teachers were to be judged severely, how much more, Christian teachers? (Matt. 23:1–33;

Mark 12:40; Luke 20:47). An examination of the condemnations of false teaching both in the Gospels and in 1 and 2 Peter and Jude show that, as with elders (1 Tim. 3; Titus 1), the lifestyle of the teacher was more important than the words he or she spoke. Teachers were primarily models, secondarily intellectual instructors. By claiming this status they put both life and words under God's scrutiny, and he would hold them responsible for misleading the flock in word or deed.

3:2 / The danger is compounded by the fact that **we all stumble in many ways.** James cites a proverb that means that Christians not only sin frequently but also sin in many ways. This truth is acknowledged throughout scripture: 2 Chron. 6:36; Job 4:17–19; Ps. 19:3; Prov. 20:9; Eccles. 7:20; Rom. 8:46; 1 John 1:8. With **if anyone is never at fault in what he says** James focuses in on the particular sin that concerns him: the wagging tongue. The need to control the tongue was well known in Judaism and Christianity (Prov. 10:19; 21:23; Eccles. 5:1; Sirach 19:16; 20:1–7). James points out here, as he did in 1:26, its importance, since a person who controls his speech **is a perfect** [person]**, able to keep his whole body in check.** That is, such a person is fully mature and complete in Christian character (1:4) and thus able to meet every test and temptation and control every evil impulse (1:12–15). As "Ben Zoma said: 'Who is mighty? He who subdues his passions,' " or, as "Alexander of Macedon asked the Elders of the South, 'Who is a hero?' They said, 'He who controls his evil passion [*yêṣer hâ-râ'*]' " (m. *Aboth* 4:1). James goes one step further than the rabbis. Control of evil impulses is good (as Paul agreed, 1 Cor. 9:24–27), but the hardest impulses to control are those of the tongue. Keep speech pure, and the rest will be "a snap"; that is the mark of the mature Christian.

3:3–4 / James illustrates his thesis "control the tongue and you can control your whole self" through a series of analogies. First, think of **horses,** which are larger and faster than humans. Yet just **put bits into the mouths of** these animals and they are controlled: not just the head, but the whole horse, is forced to go wherever the rider wishes. A second analogy is to **ships.** Ships were one of the largest structures early Christians knew.

Even a small fishing vessel was impressive; how much more so an ocean-going transport. Far more impressive were the forces driving them, winds before which trees bend and clouds move. Yet for all this size and power a small, tongue-shaped rudder (small at least in comparison with the ship or the wind) could be moved by the pilot at the tiller and the ship's course changed. Both are striking analogies of "control the tongue, control the whole."

James has shifted his argument somewhat through his illustrations. He began by saying, "If you can control the tongue, you are such a spiritual giant that you *will* also *be able* to control the rest of the body." His illustrations speak more to the point, "If you control the tongue, you *will* control the rest of the body." But this shift allows James to move on to his awareness that the tongue often incites the person to action: First you give voice to a forbidden idea, and then you give physical expression to it; first you get into a deep discussion or argument, then you commit adultery or murder. It is to this power of the tongue that James now turns, but both ideas, the difficulty of controlling speech and the fantastic power of speech, are continually playing back and forth in his mind.

3:5 / Likewise the tongue is a small part of the body, but it makes great boasts: The tongue is indeed small, but what great events for good or evil it can claim credit for! And how frequently the events are evil and the boasting proud; the very use of the term **boasts** reminds the reader of Paul's frequent condemnation of any boasting other than boasting in Christ (Rom. 1:30; 3:27; 11:18; 2 Cor. 10:13–16; Eph. 2:9). The tongue is like **a small spark**, which can set a **great forest** on fire, whether the forest is Palestinian scrub, dried to explosive tinder by the long dry season, or a California mountainside. A fire is left unguarded or a match is dropped; the action can never be taken back, for with a whoosh and roar it is soon eating up acres at a galloping pace.

3:6 / The tongue also is a fire: With this James begins to pile up almost psychedelic portraits of the evil in the tongue.

As **a fire** it is destructive. One need only think of the oratory of
an Adolf Hitler to underscore this point. Not only is the tongue
destructive, but it is **a world of evil**; or, as an alternative translation has it, "the unrighteous world." This unrighteous world is
occupying its place **among the parts of the body. It corrupts the
whole person**. The world is something that the Christian usually
thinks of as "out there." James points to his open mouth and says,
"The world is in here." The uncontrolled tongue is the embodi-
ment and seat of the evil impulse in the body. And it is not limited in its effect to its own area, for it spreads **evil** or stains the
whole body: The whole person is tarred by the brush of his or her
tongue. Yet judgment awaits even the casual word (Matt. 12:36).

Furthermore, it **sets the whole course of his life on fire,
and is itself set on fire by hell**. The problem with words is that
they do not stop there: They have serious effects. "Sticks and
stones can break my bones, but words can never hurt me" is pro-
foundly false biblically. The flame of the tongue catches the passion: A temper rises, a lust is inflamed. Soon the words, whether
an internal dialogue unheard outside or actual speech, burst forth
into action. The emotions, the whole of the body, are uncontrol-
lably involved. And where does this destructive fire originate?
From **hell** itself! Here the prison of Satan and the demons stand,
by metonymy, for the prisoners. Is that argument inspired by
God's Spirit? No. It is inspired, but by the devil himself. The
flames of hate and prejudice, of jealousy, slander, and envy lick
straight up from the lake of fire.

3:7–8 / Having said some rather strong things about the
tongue, James now turns to arguing his case in detail. His main
point will be that the tongue, that is, human speech, is hopelessly
evil. He begins with an analogy from nature: "**All kinds of** species **are being tamed and have been tamed by** humans." He is
not arguing scientifically: It would not bother him to learn that
no one had yet tamed a rhinoceros or that in his day killer whales
still lacked human contact; nor is James concerned about whether
an animal is fully domesticated. It is enough for him that wild-
cats and apes can be brought under human control. This is true,
from the prisoner taming the mice and rats in his dungeon, to

the elephant driver causing his beast to lift an Indian prince, to the snake charmer in the market and the merchant with birds that fly to him on command. This had been true in the past (**have been tamed**), but it is not part of some golden age half-forgotten—it is present experience as well (**are being tamed**). Furthermore, this truth is applicable to all the four major classes of animals: **animals** (i.e., mammals), **birds, reptiles** (which includes amphibians), and **creatures of the sea**.

But what a contrast when one comes to the tongue! **No** one **can tame the tongue**: The problem of controlling speech was a byword of the Greek and Hebrew cultures: It was a maxim that James hardly needed to prove. Did not his readers have dozens of things they wished they could "unsay" or many words they had spoken in error? Had they not learned dozens of proverbs to try to help them: "Reckless words pierce like a sword, but the tongue of the wise brings healing" (Prov. 12:18); "He who guards his lips guards his life, but he who speaks rashly will come to ruin" (Prov. 13:3). Surely James' words are self-evident to every honest person.

Instead of being tamed, the tongue **is a restless** (or unstable) **evil**. As Hermas would later say, "Defamation is evil; it is a restless demon, never at peace, but always dwells in dissension" (*Mandate* 2.3). In contrast, God is perfectly single-minded, stable, and at peace, "For God is not a God of disorder [confusion, restlessness, instability] but of peace" (1 Cor. 14:33). Yet speech is frequently characterized by instability; one believes one has controlled the tongue, then in an unguarded moment a critical, defamatory word slips out. Uncontrollable, restless, unstable—those are also the characteristics of the demonic, as James will soon point out (3:16).

Furthermore, the tongue is **full of deadly poison**. The psalmist agreed: "They make their tongues as sharp as a serpent's; the poison of vipers is on their lips" (Ps. 140:3). The comparison with snakes was widespread in Jewish literature, perhaps because the tongue looks a bit like a snake, perhaps because a snake kills with the mouth, and perhaps because the serpent in Eden deceived with its smooth words. There is no evidence that James is depending on any particular passage; he is simply asserting that words are not harmless; they are dangerous, as deadly as poison if they are not controlled. This is James' answer to the modern tendency to see words as unimportant and cheap.

3:9 / Having asserted the evil in the tongue and the difficulty of controlling it, James now gives some concrete examples of its uncontrollable nature. First of all, **we praise our Lord and Father.** Every reader would agree. Blessing or thanking God for his goodness was a part of the liturgical life of every Jew and Christian: They chanted (called "singing") psalms such as Psalm 31:21 or 103:1, 2; they had morning and evening prayers of blessing in which God was thanked for protection during the night and the good of the day (the prayers of Acts 2:42); and there were the thanksgivings over each meal: "Blessed art thou, O, Lord God of our fathers, who gives us the fruit of the ground. . . ."

Unfortunately, the tongue is also used to **curse men.** Scripture abounds with curses, although it limits cursing and is at best uneasy about it: Genesis 9:25; 49:7; Judges 9:20; Proverbs 11:26. Curses were common because, like blessings, they not only vented emotion, but also really affected the person or things against which they were directed. Although Paul forbids casual cursing (Rom. 12:14), in practice he utters some curselike words (1 Cor. 5:1; 16:22; Gal. 1:8). Jude is virtually a long curse against heretics. Yet these more formal curses on people who do certain things are hardly the curse of anger, jealousy, or rivalry used as a weapon to separate or reject groups within the church in interparty strife, much less the casual curse of someone with a personal grudge.

James points out the inconsistency of such cursing by adding, **who have been made in God's likeness.** Although a saying of Jesus forbidding cursing may be his deeper emotional basis (e.g., Luke 6:28), James uses instead this theological argument to drive home the inconsistency of the action. The Old Testament refers to humans as made in **God's likeness** (Gen. 1:26), and it uses that fact to argue about the seriousness of defacing that likeness (Gen. 9:6). Even the most depraved human bears God's likeness, and the likeness in biblical thought was seen as representing the person it depicted. To bless or thank God and then to turn around and curse his likeness is like praising a king to his face and then smashing the head off his statue as one leaves the palace. At best it is inconsistent; at root it shows uncontrolled, unrepented evil lurking within that the person does not dare show toward God but vents on people instead. James, however, sympathetically recognized the unstable nature in people and identifies with it by using **we**, not because he accepts it as appropriate, but because in leading people to repentance he wishes to show them a better way (3:13–18).

3:10 / The obvious problem here is the fickleness of speech: **Out of the same mouth come praise and cursing. My brothers, this should not be**. The problem is not so much that of blessing and cursing per se—one might, for example, curse sin quite properly: "May every angry thought that would invade my mind be buried in the depths of hell!" The problem is that both cursing and blessing are directed at the same object: God and a person-in-the-image-of-God. That shows double-thought and thus sinfulness. It is specifically this duality of speech (the "he speaks with forked tongue" of American idiom) that biblical tradition rejects (e.g., Ps. 62:4). This rejection was carried on in later Judaism (the apocryphal work Sirach 5:19 speaks of the "double-tongued sinner") and Christianity (e.g., Didache 2:4, "Do not be double-minded nor double-tongued, for the double tongue is a snare of death"). So James is on the same theme he mentions in 1:8 and 4:8—doubleness, fickleness, instability, are a sign of the evil impulse and must not be tolerated. The Christian is called to root out all such tendencies and to arrive at singleness and sincerity of heart.

3:11–12 / James concludes his argument with more analogies from nature: **Can both fresh water and salt water flow from the same spring?**. This was an unfortunate truth all around the Mediterranean, whether in the Lycus valley (Rev. 3:15–16 refers to the water supply of the area), Marah in Sinai (Exod. 15:23–25), or the Jordan rift valley, where the water cascading down a cliff would be such a welcome sight until a traveler discovered it was bitter. Why should humans try to do what springs do not? The analogy between the mouth of a spring and the human mouth fits very well.

Second, **My brothers, can a fig tree bear olives, or a grapevine bear figs?** Again the analogy fits. No tree bears two species

of fruit. Each produces according to its nature. It is unnatural for
a human to try to do what nature does not. Yet perhaps James
means something more, for Jesus used a similar illustration (Matt.
7:16–20; Luke 6:43–45; Matt. 12:33–35), but this one dealt with
good and *bad* fruit and judging a plant by its fruit. Is James suggesting that the bad fruit (the cursing) reveals the nature of the
person?

The third analogy confirms the suspicion: **Neither can a salt
spring produce fresh water.** James has shifted his analogy. Now
the spring is clearly bad, salty, but still is trying to produce sweet
water. That is impossible. The evil within the person produces
an "inspiration," which is frequently well hidden, but the "curses"
(criticism, slander, negative remarks) mixed with the pious language show the real source of inspiration. The teacher or the
Christian claims God's Spirit or God's wisdom, but is that true?
It is not true if the person's language reveals that he or she is really
a salty spring trying to be sweet.

Having argued above for the danger inherent in the tongue
and the need for purity in speech, James now moves behind
speech to the motives inspiring it. This section looks two ways.
On the one hand, it looks back to the teachers of 3:1 and the real
problems underlying impure speech in general. On the other
hand, it is a bridge between the theoretical discussion of 3:1–13
and the denunciation of the problems in the community of 4:1–
12. Just as there were two births, two inspirations, in 1:12–18, so
there are two "wisdoms," two Spirits, here.

3:13 / James has already argued for simple, sincere
speech; now he makes an appeal. **Who is wise and understanding among you?** At one level this is a question that simply asks
if someone fits the description, but at a deeper level one remem-
bers that 1 Corinthians 1–3 describes a church in which rival teachers claimed superior wisdom, and perhaps that was happening
in James' community as well. At the least, he knows that the
teachers of 3:1 were claiming to be understanding, for how else
could they teach? It is such persons, as well as those who aspire
to understanding, whom James addresses.

How are such persons to **show** their wisdom? By clever refu-
tation of those who disagree with their position? By no means;

rather, show it **by** [their] **good life**. Jesus had taught that one
would know true teachers from false ones by how they lived
(Matt. 7:15–23). James is applying his master's teaching. Lifestyle
was absolutely critical for the early church. Elders were primarily
examples (1 Pet. 5:3; 1 Tim. 4:12; 2 Tim. 3:10–11), secondarily
teachers: Their qualifications stress their exemplary lives and only
mention their teaching ability as one item among many (1 Tim.
3; Titus 1). Lifestyle was an important witness as well (1 Pet. 2:12;
3:2, 16), for if it did not succeed in converting, it at least removed
the excuses from the mouths of unbelievers at the final judgment. James states that not one's orthodoxy (right preaching) but
one's orthopraxis (right living) is the mark of true wisdom. One
must reject the teacher who does not live like Jesus; one discounts
the profession that does not lead to holiness.

James stresses two marks of this lifestyle. The first is good
deeds. Actions do speak louder than words (Matt. 5:16). The
works one does show where the heart is really invested (e.g.,
Matt. 6:19–21, 24). James commends such practices as charity and
caring for widows as marks of wisdom.

The second mark is performing these deeds **in the humility
that comes from wisdom**. Unlike the hypocrites of Matthew 6:1–
5, the truly wise know how to act out of humility: They are not
building their own reputations. Like Moses (Num. 12:3) and Jesus
(Matt. 11:29; 21:5; 2 Cor. 10:1), they are not interested in defend-
ing themselves. They avoid conflict and especially avoid adver-
tising themselves. Humility is the mark of the truly wise.

3:14 / On the other hand, if instead of being marked by
a holy lifestyle, meekness, and good deeds, the Christian is
marked by a heart that harbors **bitter envy and selfish ambition**,
that is another matter. All of these adjectives describe conditions
in your hearts, and they describe them from God's standpoint.
The person might not let these characteristics rise to conscious-
ness in undisguised form. The **envy** James names is "harsh zeal"
or "rivalry"; the same term can have a positive meaning of
"zealous" elsewhere in scripture (e.g., 1 Kings 19:10), and surely
the person so characterized is persuaded this is the case. But in
reality it is a rigidity arising from personal pride. **Bitter** is an adjective describing the envy, and is not the loving and firm zeal of

someone intoxicated by God but a "zeal" deeply tinged with bitterness. Whatever lofty motives are proclaimed, the very harshness in the tone and the cynicism displayed toward opponents reveal the real jealousy.

With these vices fits **selfish ambition**, which is better translated "party spirit" (Gal. 5:20; 2 Cor. 12:20). In the grip of rivalry, the leader feels he or she must withdraw in some way to "witness to the truth" that the main group of Christians has rejected. Here is a very sensitive issue, for church history does know of groups driven out or withdrawing in pain and sadness as a witness to the truth; there were times this was necessary. But too often what begins as a witness gets subtly invaded by rivalry, which leads to a split.

If these vices characterize your heart, **do not boast about it or deny the truth**. Better translated this would be "don't lie against the truth." People may claim, in the teeth of James' evidence, to be filled with God's Spirit. James pleads with them not to aggravate their problem by continuing to assert that God motivates their rivalry. By boasting in their zeal or arguing endlessly the rightness of their cause, they bring the cause of the kingdom into disrepute and further blind their own eyes.

3:15 / The jealous person is not inspired by God: **such "wisdom" does not come down from heaven**. James did believe wisdom came from God (1:5), for it is one of his good gifts (1:17). Jewish teaching also connected wisdom to the gift or presence of God's Spirit (e.g., Gen. 41:38–39; Exod. 31:3–4; Prov. 2:6; 8:22–31). Thus one could paraphrase James as "this behavior is not inspired by God's Spirit."

What, then, is the source and character of this "wisdom" that inspires them? First, it **is earthly**. On the surface, to say that something belongs to the earth is not bad, but it is bad if the something is claimed to come from God (1 Cor. 15:40). Thus James already argues that their inspiration is at best their own natural selves. Second, it is **unspiritual**, or "soulish." The term is used in the New Testament for the person who does not have God's Spirit (Jude 19) or who "does not accept the things that come from the Spirit of God" (1 Cor. 2:14). This "wisdom," then, is not from their redeemed natures, but characterizes those to whom the true ways of the Spirit are foreign. The ways of the world—power, command (cf. Mark 10:45), strategy, prerogatives—are what such a one understands, not meekness, love, self-giving. Third, it is **of the devil**. There is an inspiration to this "wisdom," but it is not godly. They claim that their rivalry is inspired. "It is inspired, all right," retorts James. "It is inspired by the devil himself!" Here James has reached the root of the matter.

3:16 / As if to clinch his argument, James continues, **For where you have envy and selfish ambition, there you find disorder and every evil practice**. The charge is not simply a "domino theory" argument, but a logical consequence of the first two vices. Rivalry and party spirit destroy the cohesiveness of the Christian community, which is built on unity and love. Once the "glue" is destroyed, all kinds of disorder and rebellion creep into the community. Furthermore, the self-assertion and independence assumed in jealous zeal destroy the ability of the community to discipline according to the apostolic tradition (Matt. 18:15–20; Gal. 5:25; 6:5). With the "brakes" of mutual reproof gone and with the need to be "accepting" for fear any criticism would lead a person to form his or her own party, it is easy to see how **every evil practice** would creep in. Community solidarity is utterly important for James, as it was for Paul (2 Cor. 12:20; Phil. 2:4), for without it moral and communal disintegration occur.

3:17 / In total contrast to the demonic "wisdom" is **the wisdom that comes from heaven**. To stress this, James lists a catalog of its virtues thatcan be compared in both form and content with Paul's catalogs for love and the Spirit (1 Cor. 13; Gal. 5:22ff.). This wisdom **is first of all pure**, which means that the person is wholly and sincerely committed to following God's moral directives; there are no crooked or unjust motives behind his or her holiness.

This purity is explained as leading to other virtues: it is **peace-loving** (as in Heb. 12:11; Prov. 3:17), which refers not to inner peace but community peace; **considerate** (Phil. 4:5; 1 Tim. 3:3; Titus 3:2), which points to a noncombative spirit; and **submissive**, which indicates a tractable or teachable spirit, a person who will gladly be corrected or learn a new truth.

Wisdom is practical, for it is **full of mercy** (the same root as the word for alms) **and good fruit,** which are the acts of charity James has already discussed (1:26–27; 2:18–26). Therefore wisdom is not primarily an intellectual concept but a practical ability to discern God's will and act accordingly.

Finally, wisdom is **impartial and sincere,** i.e. free from prejudice. It is unclear whether this freedom from prejudice refers to a lack of party spirit (impartiality in receiving fellow Christians) or whether it means "having a single outlook," "unwavering" (the opposite of 1:6–8). Perhaps it means the latter, since it comes next to "sincere" or "not hypocritical" (the Greek term is the latter, which implies the NIV translation of "sincere"). Together the two terms indicate people whose inner motives are sincere and whose outward acts are consistent. One need never doubt "where they are coming from," for they are nonpartisan in that they act the same toward all people.

3:18 / James summarizes his argument with a proverb: **Peacemakers who sow in peace raise a harvest or righteousness.** The harvest of goodness or righteousness is well known in biblical literature (e.g., Isa. 32:16–18; Amos 6:12). In other words, good deeds will be produced by the actions of peacemakers. Some people try to be righteous in such a way that it splits a community. The proverb instead points to goodness as the natural fruit of a peacemaker's life, and that is James' point: peacemaking, not a harsh "striving for the truth," leads to righteousness. The repetitious **sow in peace** simply underlines the fact that peacemaking is an activity producing true, outward peace. James himself is portrayed as a peacemaker in Acts 15 and 21, but his teaching comes not from his personal preference but from Jesus, who said, "Blessed are the peacemakers." (Matt 5:9). Conflict and combat will not produce justice; the way to justice is peace. Indeed, true peace in the community will be the result of doing justice to everyone.

Additional Notes   §3

3:1 / The teaching office developed from Judaism, in which, even in the New Testament period before formal rabbinic ordination came into being (after A.D. 70), people were honored with the title "rabbi" (Matt. 8:19; John 1:38), "scribe" (Matt. 2:4), "teacher" (Luke 2:46), or "teacher of the Law" (Luke 5:17). The early Christian communities also needed instruction in both the Old Testament and the Christian way of life, even more so as new converts poured into the church. At times this office was thought of as scribal (Matt. 13:52), but usually the term was "teacher." They were highly valued along with prophets, for whereas one spoke by direct inspiration from God and the other explained and applied scripture and the growing Christian tradition, both brought God's message (Acts 13:1 and Didache 13:2 include them with prophets, as does Paul in 1 Cor. 12:28). That such a powerful office attracted the unfit is not only true of the New Testament period (1 Tim. 6:3; 1 Pet. 2:1; 1 John 3) but also later in the early church: "But they praise themselves for having understanding [which they lack in reality] and wish to be teachers on an unofficial basis, though foolish as they are. So because of this haughtiness many, by exalting themselves, have been ruined, for self-determination and overconfidence are a great demon" (Hermas *Similitudes* 9.22.2–3).

The teaching of the severer judgment of teachers was traditional in the church, for James can say **you know** (as in Rom. 5:3; 6:9; Eph. 6:8). Paul considered himself a teacher, as James also did, and he like James took future judgment seriously, in light of which he disciplined himself (1 Cor. 9:27).

See further J. Jeremias, *Jerusalem in the Time of Jesus*, pp. 241–45; S. S. Laws, *James*, pp. 140–43; K. Wegenast, "Teacher," *NIDNTT*, vol. 3, pp. 766–68.

3:2 / James uses an unusual word for **stumble**, used only four times in the New Testament; see also James 2:10; Rom. 11:11; 2 Pet. 1:10. The word literally means "to stumble" or "trip," but when applied to moral issues, as here, it means "to go astray" or "to sin" or even "to be ruined or lost."

This whole passage is tied together by catchwords. **Stumble** ties the proverb to the rest of the verse. **Keep in check** is literally "to bridle" and thus links to "bit" in verse 3, which is similar in spelling in Greek.

His whole body: the body was viewed as the seat of the passions, the evil impulse.

3:3–4 / Because the illustrations do not fit exactly, some have felt there is an allegorical meaning (B. Reicke, *James*, p. 37) or that James has borrowed from other literature (M. Dibelius, *James*, pp. 185–90). It is quite possible that James is quoting popular proverbs, for surely there were plenty of popular sayings about horses and ships in those days. But to posit a rather forced allegorical meaning or a literary source without an exact literary parallel pushes the evidence too far. It may just be that James' mind is jumping ahead of itself and he is using the illustrations as a bridge to his next thought. At any rate, horse and ship illustrations were too widespread for James to need to have found one in a *written* source.

3:5 / The second half of this verse is probably a proverb used as a transition to the new point James will make about the tongue, namely, the evil in it.

3:6 / The likening of the tongue to **fire** has an Old Testament background: Pss. 10:7; 39:1–3; 83:14; 120:2–4; Prov. 16:27; 26:21; Isa. 30:27. Sirach, commenting in a long passage on slander, states, "[The tongue] will not be master over the godly, and they will not be burned in its flame" (28:22; cf. Psalms of Solomon 12:2–3).

The structure of this verse is difficult, for the grammar is unclear; but the general sense is clear. The **world** is a symbol for the culture and institutions of the universe as organized without God and thus the antithesis of the kingdom of God; James always uses it with this meaning (1:27; 2:5; 4:4), and the adjectival phrase "unrighteous" clinches this meaning. James is very close to 1 John in his thought, although different in style. See further J. Guhrt, "Earth," *NIDNTT*, vol. 1, pp. 524–26 or H. Sasse, "*Kosmos*," *TDNT*, vol. 3, pp. 868–96.

That the world occupies its place **among the parts of the body** may be a reference to the evil impulse (Hebrew *yêṣer hâ-râ'*), first cited in James 1:13, which the Jews spoke of as living in one's members. In that case James is picturing it as living in the tongue, but this is hardly a full statement of his anthropology. His language is partly metaphorical and means much the same as Jesus' when he says that corruption is not outside but inside the person, that evil comes from the heart (Mark 7:14–23). James is dealing with community strife, prejudice, and rejection of the call to give. He pictures this as residing in the tongue, but as with Jesus, the defilement within stains not the tongue alone but the **whole person**. A similar image is in Jude 23 (cf. Wisdom 15:4).

The phrase **the whole course of** [one's] **life** has occasioned much discussion, for it is similar to Orphic and other Greek expressions for reincarnation. But the expression is so widespread in later Greek literature, with such varying meanings, that one must conclude that by James' time it had lost its connection to Orphic teaching and had taken on in Palestine a meaning like the GNB translation. See further J. B. Adamson, *James*, p. 160–64.

The reference to **hell** is interesting. Hell, or Gehenna, was apparently thought of by James and others as the place where the demons and Satan were already imprisoned (as opposed to future imprisonment in Rev. 19–20). This is clearly the sense of the Jewish work the

Apocalypse of Abraham 14:31. But the image in this passage is not just one of imprisoned beings but of beings able to inspire present events, like those in Rev. 9:1–11; 20:7–8. Apparently the prison is used as a graphic image for those who will live or are living there, particularly because of the flame imagery associated with it. See further J. Jeremias, *"Geenna,"* *TDNT*, vol. 1, pp. 657–58.

3:7 / The only other place the word **tame** appears in the New Testament is in Mark 5:4, where demons make a man untamable.

The four classes of animals are the four common divisions of the animal world in biblical literature, which classified by observed groupings, not modern taxonomic categories. See Gen. 1:26; 9:2; Deut. 4:17–18; Acts. 10:12; 11:6.

3:8 / There is a massive amount of material on the tongue in scripture (e.g., Prov. 10:20; 15:2, 4; 21:3; 31:26) and also in intertestamental literature (e.g., Sirach 14:1; 19:6; 25:8).

The term **restless** is the same word that appeared in 1:8 ("undecided") and that appears frequently in the New Testament as a noun meaning "restlessness," "instability," "tumult." God's characteristic is peace, the normal antonym to this term, not instability, Luke 21:9; 2 Cor. 6:5; 12:20. This contrast will come out clearly in the following verses and in 3:13–18. See further H. Beck and C. Brown, "Peace," *NIDNTT*, vol. 2, p. 780.

On the **poison** image in Jewish literature, see Job 5:15; Ps. 58:4, 5; Sirach 28:17–23. Hermas *Similitude* 9.26.7 reads, "For just as wild beasts destroy and kill a man with their poison, so also the words of such men destroy and kill a man." See further O. Michel, *"Ios,"* *TDNT*, vol. 3, pp. 334–35.

3:9 / Thanking or blessing was frequently directed toward God (Matt. 11:25), so that God can be referred to simply as "the Blessed One" (Mark 14:61; Rom. 9:5); the rabbis normally referred to God as "the Holy One, blessed be He." In the New Testament prayers frequently blessed or thanked God (Luke 1:68; 2 Cor. 1:3; Eph. 1:3; 1 Pet. 1:3), as did the Jewish Eighteen Benedictions used at the end of every synagogue service. In fact, God is the normal object of blessing in the New Testament, although on occasion people are blessed (e.g., Matt. 16:17). In the Lord's Supper the blessing of God for food was applied to the special food of bread and wine: Neither at a daily meal nor at the weekly Lord's Supper was the food blessed, but as Jesus did at the Last Supper, God was blessed or thanked for the food. In Didache 9:2, 3, "We thank you, our Father, for . . . " is repeated concerning the cup and the bread, showing this to be the practice of the early church. See further H. G. Link, "Blessing," *NIDNTT*, vol. 1, pp. 206–15.

The title **Lord and Father** has no exact parallel in Jewish literature (1 Chron. 29:10 and Isa. 63:16 are the closest). It is probably a current expression of the church, combining the Lord (*Kyrios*) of the synagogue with Jesus' favorite address to God in prayer.

It is clear that curses were used in the Old Testament (cf. also Prov. 24:24; Eccles. 7:21; Sirach 4:5). In the rabbinic literature the Jews also rejected cursing, for the same reason James does—people are made in God's image. The Secrets of Enoch states: "The Lord with his hands having created man in the likeness of his own face, the Lord made him small and great. Whoever reviles the ruler's face . . . has despised the Lord's face, and he who vents anger on any man . . . the Lord's great anger will cut him down" (44:1-3). Yet the Jews' rejection of cursing did not cover the formal liturgical curses of the Eighteen Benedictions. Apparently, in the New Testament similar formal curses directed at anyone who did *x or y* were acceptable. Paul never curses his adversaries, even the Judaizers; neither does he accuse them of doing what he curses. Paul's were more formal "if the shoe fits, wear it" curses, not personal, rash, or occasional ones.

3:10 / The rejection of doubleness is an important concept for James, as the note on 1:8 shows. He has surely read Sirach 28:12, "If you blow on a spark, it will glow; if you spit on it, it will be put out; and both come out of your mouth." This is set in a wider context of Sirach 27:30–28:26. In 28:13 the double-tongued ("the deceiver," RSV) is roundly cursed. Testament of Benjamin 6:5 reads, "The good mind hath not two tongues, of blessing and of cursing . . . but it hath one disposition, uncorrupt and pure, concerning all men." In essence, whether one looks in Jewish or Christian works of the early period, the mere appearance of a double attitude (which is not just the honest admission that "I have not made up my mind yet") is an indication of the sinful disposition.

J. B. Mayor, *James*, p. 123, believes the logic of this passage means that one should never curse a human. That is true, although James would most likely not have drawn this conclusion. Still it is not unusual for a New Testament teaching to have implications beyond New Testament practice, as, for example, in the case of slavery. In 2 Pet. 2:10–11 and Jude 8–10 this principle is extended to reject even the idea of cursing evil powers, including Satan.

3:11–12 / Any geologically active area will have sweet and bitter springs. In the Lycus valley, Hierapolis had hot mineral springs, Colossae cool, sweet springs; Laodicea had to put up with lukewarm water piped in from a distance. In the Jordan valley the traveler would have to guess which of several springs seen in the distance were sweet and travel miles accordingly. See further E. F. F. Bishop, *Apostles of Palestine*, p. 187; or D. Y. Hadidian, "Palestinian Pictures in the Epistle of James," p. 228.

The King James Version reads, "So can no fountain both yield salt water and fresh"; this reading follows an inferior Greek text that harmonized 3:12 with 3:11. The NIV follows a better text and thus shows James' shifting thought, making a good transition to the next section.

3:13 / The word-pair **wise and understanding** is frequently found in the Old Testament (Deut. 1:13, 15; 4:6; Dan. 5:12); it indicates a people living according to God's insight.

Lifestyle is important throughout the New Testament, e.g., Heb. 13:7; Gal. 1:13. Paul constantly states that lifestyle marks the unregenerate from the regenerate (e.g., Gal. 5). The Jews likewise insisted that lifestyle was important: "[R. Eleazar ben Azariah] used to say: Everyone whose wisdom is greater than his deeds, to what is he like? To a tree whose branches are many and its roots few; and the wind comes out and roots it up and turns it over on its face" (m. *Aboth* 3:22).

The Greeks felt meekness and **humility** were vices. Christians believed they were cardinal virtues (Gal. 5:23; 6:1; Eph. 2:4; 2 Tim. 2:25; Titus 3:2; 1 Pet. 3:15). Thus James as a Christian opposes his self-assertive culture. See further S. S. Laws, *James*, pp. 160–61.

3:14 / There are many places where the Greek word *zēlos* (**envy,** zeal) is translated positively (John 2:17; Rom. 10:2; 2 Cor. 7:7; 11:2; Phil. 3:6). But this virtue easily merges into jealousy and rivalry, which the same word condemns in vice lists (Acts 5:17; 13:45; Rom. 10:2; 13:13; 1 Cor. 3:3). James seems to indicate that the moment one senses even a hint of a bitter spirit, it is time to examine one's true motivations. See further A. Stumpff, "*Zēlos,*" *TDNT*, vol. 2, pp. 887–88.

The problem of party spirit was well known in the early church. The first indications are in Acts 6; then follow the Galatian Judaizers, the groups in Corinth (1 Cor. 1), and other unknown groups (Phil. 1:17; 2:3). This is a chief vice in the New Testament, for in a group founded on a truth that tended to separate it from mainline Judaism, many would lose sight of the fact that the truth was a *person* who unified them and instead so focus on their little truths that they distorted them and then persuaded themselves that withdrawal was necessary. See further F. Büchsel, "*Eritheia,*" *TDNT*, vol. 2, pp. 660–61.

James 3:13–18 is a modified vice and virtue list, of which there are many in the New Testament. Didache 1–6 and Barnabas 18–21 are similar lists in later Christian literature. All, like James, trace sin back to **your hearts**, rather than to external forces. See further B. S. Easton, "New Testament Ethical Lists."

3:15 / Paul can speak of a "wisdom of this world" (1 Cor. 1:20; 2:6) or a "human wisdom" (fleshly wisdom; 2 Cor. 1:12), but James never does, for wisdom is his term for the Holy Spirit. The link between wisdom and heaven had already been forged in Jewish teaching (e.g., Sirach 1:1–4; 24:1–12; Wisdom 7:24–27; 9:4, 6, 9–18), as had the link between wisdom and the Spirit (Wisdom 7:7, 22–23 speaks of "the spirit of wisdom" and of a "spirit that is intelligent, holy" in her). James simply makes use of the identifications in a more concrete way. See further J. A. Kirk, "The Meaning of Wisdom in James."

The term **earthly** normally indicates at least inferiority (John 3:12; Phil. 3:19; 2 Cor. 5:1), but it is the weakest of the terms, which are arranged in ascending order. Hermas, in meditating on James, has strengthened the idea: " 'So you see,' he said, 'that faith is from above, from the Lord, and has great power; but double-mindedness is an earthly spirit from the devil, which has no power ' " (*Mandate* 9.11).

The term **of the devil** has already been suggested by "lying against the truth" (3:14), which characterizes the devil (John 8:46). Because James later calls on people to *resist* the devil (4:7) and because of the connection between testing and the devil (e.g., Matt. 6:13) to which Hermas also witnesses (*Similitude* 9.12; 9.23.5), it is unlikely James is simply saying they were doing things *like* the devil but rather saying that they were inspired by him.

3:16 / The First Letter of John is also deeply concerned about sectarian behavior (1 John 2:19). The scripture recognizes the need for separation from the world, but it rejects divisions among true Christians.

That demons would be involved in **every evil practice** (cf. John 3:20; 5:29, which use the same term) is not surprising. Yet **disorder** is the primary mark of demonic activity. God is the author of peace and order (1 Cor. 14:33). The demonic realm is characterized by restlessness and rebellion (cf. Luke 21:9 and the comments on James 1:8; 3:8). See further A. Oepke, "*Akatastasia,*" *TDNT,* vol. 3, pp. 446–47.

3:17 / Hermas, *Mandate* 9.8 has a catalog with a structure similar to this catalog in James that also stresses peace.

The terms **submissive** and **impartial** are found in biblical literature only here.

The term **sincere** ("not hypocritical") has a massive biblical background: Rom. 12:9; 2 Cor. 6:6; 1 Tim. 1:5; 2 Tim. 1:5; 1 Pet. 1:22.

3:18 / **Harvest of righteousness** is literally the "fruit of righteousness." See also Prov. 11:30; 2 Cor. 9:10; Phil. 1:11; Heb. 12:11. Scripture and related literature also knows "the fruit of wisdom" (Sirach 1:16) and "the fruit of the Spirit" (Gal. 5:20). Goodness or righteousness is justice, where all get their due.

Some, e.g., S. S. Laws, *James,* pp. 165–66, connect wisdom to the fruit of righteousness and thus say peacemakers possess wisdom, for peace is the mark of its presence. Laws cites Prov. 11:30 and 3:18 as evidence. This is a possible interpretation, but not the most natural one. See further F. Hauck, "*Karpos,*" *TDNT,* vol. 3, p. 615; H. Beck and C. Brown, "Peace," *NIDNTT,* vol. 2, pp. 776–83.

§4 *The Christian and the World (James 4:1–12)*

Because he is aware of practical problems in the community, James makes an abrupt switch from peacemakers, the wise leaders of the community, to the actual situation of intrachurch conflict.

4:1 / **What causes fights and quarrels among you?** That is a good question, for if God's wisdom is found in peacemakers, community strife does not come from them. A conflict with the pagan world or the synagogue might be the inevitable result of following Christian standards, but these are quarrels within the church (i.e., **among you**); civil war, not national defense.

James asks the question rhetorically, for he knows the answer: **Don't they come from your desires?** As in 1:13–15, he will not blame external forces: the source is their own evil impulses or, as Paul would say, the old (or fleshly) nature. Their quarrels may be "only human," but this is fallen humanity; until they recognize and repent of their sin, there is no hope for peace in the church.

The real battleground, then, is internal: The desires continually **battle within you**. The evil impulses in a person are not a part of the body (which can serve God as easily as evil) but are in the body and fight to control it. In theory, given the Spirit or "the wisdom from above," people should be able to conquer these impulses, but given the fact that their allegiance is divided between God and the world (James 4:4, 8), there is no victory for these people but only a constant struggle between the part of them God has and the part controlled by the world. The language is graphic; the struggle is a deep experience.

4:2 / The results of their failure are also graphically described. Though the NIV translation is a faithful interpretation of one way of reading the text, a better translation is the following:

> You want things that you are not able to have;
> You "murder" and are jealous, but you cannot get your desires;
> You quarrel and fight and you do not have what you want because you do not ask God for it:
> You ask, and you do not receive it because your motives are bad.

James is arguing in more detail the statement he made in 4:1. The root of conflict is desire: You want something. This is precisely the issue in 1:14. Whatever the object, desire is the origin of sin and conflict. Furthermore, James points out the consequences when desire is frustrated (you **don't get** what **you want**). Rather than reexamine the desire, the person in its grip resorts to slander and verbal abuse of those who do have ("murder" in the metaphorical sense). This is accompanied by jealousy (as in 3:14), which may appear friendly on the surface but masks a struggle for power. Personal rivalry leads to party struggles: **You quarrel and fight**. The words of 3:16 have come true in the community: it is full of disorder. Yet even with all the intrigue, the end result is not obtained: **You do not have** [what you want].

They have tried to satisfy desire the wrong way, but the Christian tradition knows a better way—asking God. It was Jesus who said, "Ask, and you will receive." They are scheming, but not asking. The result is frustration.

4:3 / Yet these Christians might respond that they do pray, but prayer seems no help at all. James' response to the implied protest is in the final line of the parallelism. **When you ask, you do not receive**, but there is a good reason for prayer's failure: **because you ask with wrong motives**. Prayer is not automatically answered. The Gospels contain many promises about prayer (Matt. 7:7–11; 17:20; Mark 11:23–24; Luke 18:1–10; John 14:13), but each of them makes a central assumption, namely, that the petitioner's heart is in tune with God's. That is what it means to pray "in the name" of Jesus, to have faith, or to ask a father for something. That is why the Lord's Prayer begins with three petitions stressing God's will. If prayer is no more than a formula (say the right words, believe hard enough, confess; it will happen), then Christians are back to a type of magic: They can manipulate God or impose their will on God, for he *has* to answer. In contrast, New Testament prayer grows out of a trusting relationship with a father whose will is supreme. James, then, can point out that they do not receive because they are not in tune with God; the reason is **you ask . . . that you may spend what you get on your pleasures**. The implication is not that God will not give us things that give us pleasure. God is the gracious God who gives not only bread and water but also steak and wine (Phil. 4:12; Jesus was not known for fasting!). The point is that they are motivated by selfish desires and ask simply to gratify themselves. This is not the trusting child asking for a meal but the greedy child asking for the best piece or the spoiled child demanding his or her way. They are asking God to bless their schemes; God will have no part of it.

4:4 / Having analyzed their plight, James adds an accusation: **you adulterous people**. This compares the people to God's Old Testament people. The church is the bride of Christ as Israel was God's bride (2 Cor. 11:2; Eph. 5:22–24; Rev. 19, 21). When Israel turned to idolatry, it did not forsake the worship of God but tried to combine the two: God in the temple, the Queen of Heaven at home; or God in the main temple, Baal in the court of the temple. Thus it is repeatedly compared to an adulterous wife, who wants to keep the security and respectability of her home and husband but also wants to enjoy her lover (Isa. 1:21; Jer. 3; Hos. 1–3). James, in applying this image to the church, accuses it of serving some "idol" as well as the Lord.

The "idol" is easily found: It is **the world. Don't you know that friendship with the world is hatred toward God? Anyone who chooses to be a friend of the world becomes an enemy of God**. The people should have recognized the fact, for the **don't you know** shows that this teaching is not new. As in 1 John 2:15–17, the world stands for human culture, mores, and structures, which are organized without God. The opposite of the world is the kingdom, of which the church is a bridgehead on this earth, in which God is the origin and center of all life. These Christians worship Christ quite faithfully, but they also seek influence, financial security, and a better standard of living, which means they cannot live the church's ideal of servanthood and generosity "too literally." Slowly the "practical" principles of the world (power, hierarchy, authority) have been brought into the church as well, as the quarrels witness.

James states flatly that this form of unfaithfulness is apostasy, just as it was in the Old Testament. The new idol according to Jesus was money or Mammon (Matt. 6:14; Luke 16:13); James says it is the world. As with Jesus, there is no "both/and." They **want friendship with the world** (which may imply that even the world does not want their halfhearted allegiance); they are therefore God's enemy. No husband will be pleased with less than an exclusive relationship; God will never accept less than total allegiance.

4:5 / To his condemnation of their behavior James adds a warning, **Or do you think Scripture says without reason that . . .** They have read the Old Testament, and only willful suppression of its message could justify their actions.

The scripture in question is probably from a lost apocryphon; the first alternative translation in the NIV is probably the correct one: **God jealously longs for the spirit that he made to live in us.** God is a jealous husband (Exod. 20:5; 34:14; Deut. 4:24), who will not tolerate adultery on the part of his "bride." The object of his jealousy is the spirit he has breathed into people (Gen. 6:17; 7:15; Ps. 104:29–30; Ezek. 37), whom he has created to worship and obey him; when instead they corrupt their spirits by serving the world, God's jealousy is aroused. Woe be to the person who ignores such a threat, as if scripture were so much paper and ink!

4:6 / James argues that God is angry with these believers; he is their enemy. Yet James leaves his readers with hope rather than dread: **But he gives us more grace.** James is aware of God's judgment upon those who refuse to repent (5:1–6), but he is equally aware of the vast readiness of God to forgive. God's desire to forgive is a precept upon which his whole book is based (5:19–20). There is reason to tremble, but trembling will be a prelude to joy if they turn to God for grace.

The proof of this truth is also found in scripture: **That is why Scripture says: "God opposes the proud, but gives grace to the humble."** This verse (Prov. 3:34) is a favorite text in the

Christian ethical tradition, and it gives people a choice: They may
humble themselves and receive God's grace, or they may continue in their self-sufficiency and experience his wrath. Not their
past sins, but their present state of heart, determines God's attitude. James' God is the gracious God of scripture.

4:7 / Since God is gracious, the next step is to repent,
which James presents in a series of ten commands. **Submit yourselves, then, to God** is the main point. If they have tried to manipulate God by their prayers, if they have ignored God's
commands in the teaching of Jesus, they have not been submitted to God. That attitude must change. There will be no cheap
grace, no forgiveness of sins in which the person intends to continue. But grace is available, if they submit.

As a first step they must halt their pleasing the devil: **Resist
the Devil, and he will flee from you.** James shows that though
the impulse to sin may be internal; to give in to that impulse is
to yield to the devil. The Gospels are clear on this point (e.g.,
Matt. 4:1–11; Mark 8:28–34; Luke 22:31; John 13:2, 27). But the
devil has no power over the Christian except the power of seduction. When resisted he must behave as he did with Jesus in
the wilderness—he fled, leaving him. That will be the experience
of the Christian as well if he or she learns to say no.

4:8 / Full repentance will mean purification. There is both
promise and demand in the call **Come near to God and he will
come near to you.** As a promise, there is the reciprocal promise of
God: Turn to him and he will turn to you (Mal. 3:7), return to him
and he will return (Zech. 1:3). God is a loving father waiting for
the chance to respond to his children in forgiveness, but the demand
states that they must repent and **come near.** This term normally indicates an activity of worship: All their church's worship is not a
coming near, for their community disharmony rooted in preoccu-
pation with worldly success makes it unacceptable. "Come near,"
calls God. "Worship me truly! Worship with obedience!" (cf. 1:27).

Continuing the metaphor, James cries, **Wash your hands,
you sinners.** Worship in the Old Testament required cultically
clean hands, so they were ritually washed before certain parts of
the worship (e.g., Exod. 30:19–21). These Christians are at present

unfit for worship because of their sin. The term **sinners** is strong, for James will not accept any excuse. Their actions are sin—plain, inexcusable sin. They will change their behavior (**wash . . . hands**) only when they accept this fact.

James moves from behavior to the inner problem when he demands: **Purify your hearts, you double-minded**. Again a ritual term from the Old Testament is selected (cf. Exod. 19:10), but the defilement now is not outward (e.g., from having touched a dead body) but inward. The nature of the purification necessary appears in the term **double-**, the same term found in 1:8, meaning, not a person consciously hiding his or her real motives but one who has divided motives. On the one hand, they wish to follow Christ and be good Christians; on the other hand, they are not willing to give up the world (cf. Rom. 6:8; 2 Cor. 5:11–17). They excuse their following worldly patterns of influence and money making (cf. 4:13–17). But James has already stated that God will not share them with the world; he wants them all (4:4). Thus they need to cleanse themselves inwardly from their worldly motives and to seek Christ and his kingdom alone.

4:9 / Proper repentance will show appropriate signs. Inwardly they should **grieve**, a "What have I done!" feeling. This inward sorrow will be expressed outwardly as they **mourn and wail**, a mark of all true revivals. Modern evangelism has tended to short-circuit this process by promising *peace* before a person has fully realized the seriousness of his or her condition. James carefully avoids that trap and calls on them to experience the seriousness of their easy acceptance of sin.

Grieving is so natural that any other response would be inappropriate: **Change your laughter to mourning and your joy to gloom**. This demand may come from Jesus' saying: "Blessed are those who mourn, for they will be comforted." (Matt. 5:4). Or, "Woe to you who laugh now, for you will mourn and weep." (Luke 6:25). Without proper repentance now, their future is bleak, but with it they will not weep later; it is in fact the only reasonable response. How could they really appreciate the seriousness of God's displeasure as James describes it and not let the smile drain from their faces and the food grow cold on the table as with tears and fasting they prostrate themselves before the Lord?

4:10 / Finally, there is hope; as they **humble** [themselves] **before the Lord**, truly regretting their sin, God's acceptance is sure: God **will lift you up** (cf. 4:6). The picture is that of someone prostrate before an oriental monarch, begging mercy. The monarch leans down from the throne and lifts the petitioner's face from the dust. The person rises with grateful joy, knowing he or she is forgiven. This metaphor occurs in the Old Testament for God's action in restoring the fortunes of the poor: "The lowly he sets on high, and those who mourn are lifted to safety" (Job 5:11). God also will not reject these Christians, if they repent and reject their sin.

James concludes his section on the tongue, wisdom, and the evil impulse with a final exhortation, which focuses on the nature of the repentance he has previously demanded.

4:11 / The paragraph break indicated by **brothers** is a welcome relief after the thundering denunciation of the last section (4:1–10). Yet James immediately gives a command, **Do not slander one another**, defining "slander" as **speak against** or **judge him**. James realizes that Christians speak negatively about other Christians: "Did you hear what she did?" It is immaterial whether the accusations are true or false, for however true the charge may be, to spread it to people uninvolved in the situation is destructive to community harmony. "Love covers over a multitude of sins" (1 Pet. 4:8). It does not broadcast sins, so Christians must not speak negatively about others.

James justifies his command not by citing Jesus, "Do not judge" (Matt. 7:1–5), but by using a reason that might bring the seriousness of the offense home more clearly: Such a critical person **speaks against the law and judges it.** In what way does the person criticize the law? The law in Leviticus 19:18 states that one should love one's neighbor as oneself. Jesus himself called this the second greatest commandment (Mark 12:31) and drew out its meaning in the golden rule (Matt. 7:12). To criticize another is neither love nor is it the way one wishes to be treated oneself. Therefore to criticize is to implicitly criticize the law itself: "It does not apply in this case." If this is true, then the one criticizing is no longer simply **keeping** the law, **but sitting in judgment on it.** Ignoring the rule about the negative comment appears innocent, but underneath it lies a spirit that is proud enough to believe that in some cases it can correct God's rules.

4:12 / James underlines his point by stating bluntly, **There is only one Lawgiver and Judge**. Jesus taught that God alone had authority to judge (John 5:22–23, 30), and every Jew knew that God gave the law. James adds, **the one who is able to save and destroy**, that is, "No one from the east or the west or from the desert can exalt a man. But it is God who judges: He brings one down, he exalts another" (Ps. 75:6–7). The two features, then, go together. God gave the law; God enforces the law. As the only sovereign, he has authority over life and death.

But you—who are you to judge your neighbor? If God gave the law, and if God is the sole judge, how dare any person set up as judge through his or her critical tongue? Criticism usurps God's authority, for as Paul states, "Who are you to judge someone else's servant? To his own Master he stands or falls. And he will stand, for the Lord is able to make him stand" (Rom. 14:4). Therefore, behind the critical spirit lies a pride that rather than humbly looking to its own need of grace usurps the role of God and sets itself up as the judge of others as if, like God's, their judgment mattered.

Additional Notes §4

4:1 / Some scholars believe the **fights and quarrels** are Jewish revolutionary activity against Rome (B. Reicke, *James*, p. 45–46). But although the words are "wars" and "battles," these were frequently used metaphorically for quarrels, e.g., 1 Clement 3:2; 2 Tim. 2:23; Titus 3:9.

The **desires** is a different term from the "evil desire" of 1:14, but it means the same. It also occurs in Luke 8:14; 2 Pet. 2:13; and Titus 3:3. The different terminology with the same meaning is evidence that the book was originally independent sermons joined together into an edited unity. See further G. Stahlin, "*Hēdonē,*" *TDNT*, vol. 2, pp. 909–26.

Within you is literally "in your members." Though some, e.g., J. H. Ropes, *James*, p. 253, believe these are the members of the church, the use of "members" elsewhere in James (3:5; 3:6), the flow of the argument, and parallels in Jewish thought all point to the bodily members of a person. Judaism believed that the evil impulse lived in the 248 members of the body (the later tradition is in *Aboth de R. Nathan* 16, but there is earlier evidence in 1 QS 4). Thus desire must be combated within the person. In 1 Pet. 2:11 the passions war against the soul, whereas in the Testament of Dan 5 they war against God. Here the soul seems undecided, and the war is between the evil impulse and wisdom (i.e., the Spirit, in Pauline or Johannine terminology).

4:2 / The original text lacked punctuation, so the exact structure is difficult to recover. Most English and American scholars have read the text as the NIV translates it, seeing it as two lines in parallel. See further S. S. Laws, *James*, p. 169; J. H. Ropes, *James*, pp. 254–55. However, there are fewer problems in Greek if the text is read as this commentary translates it, four lines of two-part parallelism arranged in a chiastic pattern (i.e., *a b b a*, two pairs of parallels). The last two lines are augmented to lead into the following topic of prayer and worldliness. See further J. B. Adamson, *James*, pp. 167–268.

The term "murder" is unusual, so some scholars argue that "murder" is a corruption in the text for "envy" (*phoneuete* instead of *phthoneite*), based upon other passages where this has happened (e.g., one manuscript of 1 Pet. 2:1) and the fact that envy and jealousy fit together (e.g., 1 Macc. 8:16; Gal. 5:21; 1 Clement 3:2; 4:7). See further J. B. Adamson, *James*, pp. 167–68. But many passages use "murder" in a metaphorical way for the sins of the tongue: "The blow of a whip raises a welt, but a blow of the tongue crushes the bones. Many have fallen by the edge of the sword, but not so many as have fallen because of the tongue" (Sirach 28:17–18; cf. 28:21). Likewise early Christians connected anger, jealousy, and murder (Didache 3:2; 1 Clement 3:4–6:3). So it is not necessary to assume a corrupt text.

The term **you covet** is the verb form of the noun used in 1:14. This is further proof that both passages speak of the same desire or evil impulse.

4:3 / The key word is **pleasures**, for it is the same word found in 4:1 ("desires [for pleasure]"—while the NIV translates it as "desires" in one verse and "pleasures" in the other, it is the same word meaning "desire for pleasure" in both cases; it is a synonym of "evil desire" in 1:14). This not only neatly closes off 4:1–3 as a section but also shows that their prayer is not a response to God, inspired by his Spirit, but a manipulating of God inspired by the evil impulse.

There has always been a problem in combining the verses that apparently promise unconditional answers to prayer (Matt. 7:7–11; 18:19–20) and those that introduce waiting (Luke 11:5–13; 18:1–8) or conditions (Matt. 17:20; 1 John 5:14, 16). Some of the problems can be solved by better exegesis, (e.g., Matt. 18:19–20 has a specific context that is often ignored), but difficulties remain. M. Dibelius, *James*, p. 219, sees the conditional verses as a response to the dashed hopes of an earlier period; but the situation is hardly so simple, for both types are found in the same literature (e.g., James has 1:5–8; 4:3; *and* 5:14–16). Actually the passages serve different functions: The unconditional ones call the believer to trust, confidence, and expectation. The conditional ones remind the lax that the promises are not magic formulae but are given to those who love God and keep his commands. Later Christian tradition tended to legalize and formularize the conditions, e.g., Hermas *Vision* 3.10.6 and *Mandate* 9.4.

See further: A. Murray, *With Christ in the School of Prayer* (Old Tappan, N.J.: Fleming H. Revell Co., 1953), esp. pp. 66–70; G. Clark, *I Will Lift Up Mine Eyes* (New York: Harper & Row, 1935), esp. the first half; R. Foster, *Celebration of Discipline,* rev. ed. (San Francisco: Harper & Row, 1978, 1988), pp. 15–61.

4:4 / **You adulterous people** is literally "adulteresses." This feminine form bothered commentators until it was realized that it paralleled the Old Testament tradition (e.g., Isa. 50:1; Jer. 13:27; Ezek. 16:38; 23:45; Hos. 9:11). The plural form is used because the church *as a whole* is seen as the faithful remnant. It is individuals who apostasized from the truth represented by the church. See further Jesus (Matt. 12:39; 16:4; Mark 8:38) and W. Eichrodt, *Theology of the Old Testament* (Philadelphia: Westminster, 1961), vol. 1, pp. 67–68, 250–58.

Paul uses "the world" as an entity in opposition to God in 1 Cor. 1–3; Eph. 2:2; Col. 2:8, but the idea is even more characteristic of John (e.g., John 13–17). Similar ideas were found in sections of Judaism with a remnant mentality: e.g., Jubilees 30:19–22; 1 Enoch 48:7; 108:8. Jesus points out in Mark 10:42–45 that the world operates on a totally different value system than the kingdom; therefore, the two cannot be combined. See further J. Wallis, *The Call to Conversion* (San Francisco: Harper & Row, 1981); J. H. Yoder, *The Politics of Jesus,* pp. 11–63, 115–62.

4:5 / Jesus also stated that all scripture would be fulfilled (Matt. 5:17–19).

The source of this **Scripture** is impossible to determine. S. S. Laws, *James,* pp. 177–79, argues that there is an allusion to Pss. 41:2 or 83:3, but neither the form of the question nor the closeness of the allusions support her translation. Others have suggested a loose sense quotation of the Old Testament or the use of a version of the Old Testament otherwise unknown. However, the **Scripture says** formula always introduces a direct quotation whenever it is used elsewhere in the New Testament. No passage has been found in any version that is identical to this quotation. That leaves one with a lost book as the probable source, which would be no more unusual than Jude's quoting 1 Enoch (Jude 14 = 1 Enoch 1:9).

The Greek of the quotation is ambiguous. The two most probable translations are **The spirit he caused to live in us tends envies intensely** (NIV text, cf. GNB: "The spirit that God placed in us is filled with fierce [or "turns toward envious"] desires") or "God jealously longs for the spirit that he made to live in us" (first NIV alternative; the second NIV alternative, "the Spirit he caused to live in us longs jealously," is less likely than either of the other two in that it has the problems of both of the others and the advantages of neither.)

The first choice does not fit the immediate context of the enmity of God but makes good sense if James is jumping back to 4:1–3 and the evil impulse. The second uses a difficult term for jealously, but as James has already used the usual term negatively in 4:2 (and 3:13–18), he may have deliberately shifted his vocabulary. Two lines of reasoning point to the second translation. First, it has Jewish precedents, for the *Fragment Targum* on Gen. 2:2 reads, "On the seventh day Yahweh's *Memra* [word] longed for the work which he had made." Other Jewish traditions also refer to the need to keep one's spirit pure: "Blessed is the man who does not defile the holy spirit of God which hath been put and breathed into him, and blessed is he who returns it to its Creator as pure as it was on the day when He entrusted it to him" (Hebrew Testament of Naphtali 10:9) Second, Christian writers interpreted James this way, for Hermas *Mandate* 3.1–2 commands truth, "so that the spirit which God caused to dwell in this flesh will be found truthful by all men" (cf. *Mandate* 5.2–5; 10.2.6; 10.3.2). See further S. S. Laws, "Does Scripture Speak in Vain?" which takes a contrary opinion; or O. J. F. Seitz, "Two Spirits in Man: An Essay in Biblical Exegesis."

4:6 / The passage from Prov. 3:34 is also used by 1 Peter to argue for mutual submission and humility in a context of resisting the devil (5:5). The passage is used in 1 Clement to argue for holiness and against slander and gossip. The need is to "join those to whom grace is given by God," and so, "let us clothe ourselves with harmony in humility and self-control" (1 Clement 30:2–3). Clement is so close to James that he has either read James or heard the same oral teaching of Jesus that James used.

4:7 / The idea of **submit** is important in scripture. First, there is submission of the creation to Jesus (based on Ps. 8:7): 1 Cor. 15:27–28; Eph. 1:22; Heb. 2:8. Then there is the submission of Christians to one another, Eph. 5:21, which is specified as the young to elders (1 Pet. 5:5), wives to husbands (Eph. 5:22), Christians to governing authorities (Rom. 13:1). Set above all there is the obedience of the Christian to God (e.g., Heb. 12:9) or to Christ (Eph. 5:24), which alone is an absolute obedience.

Resist the devil is in 1 Pet. 5:8–9 and Eph. 6:13. It is common in the Testaments of the Twelve Patriarchs (e.g., Simeon 3:3; Dan 5:1; Asher 3:3). The Christian writer Hermas adds, " '[The devil] cannot,' he said, 'dominate the servants of God who hope in him with all their hearts. The devil can wrestle, but he cannot pin. If, then, you resist him, he will flee defeated from you in disgrace' " (*Mandate* 5.2). The means of resistance, then, are good works (in the Testaments) or total commitment to God (Hermas). See further H. Berkhof, *Christ and the Powers* (Scottdale, Penn.: Herald Press, 1962); or C. Williams, *Descent of the Dove* (Grand Rapids: Wm. B. Eerdmans, 1939).

4:8 / The cultic act **come near** is seen in the Old Testament (e.g., Exod. 19:22; 24:2; Deut. 16:16; Pss. 122, 145), where the worshiper actually approached the theophany (such as Moses at the burning bush) or the temple (where God lived), an action that presupposed previous cultic purification (cf. 2 Chron. 26:16–20, King Uzziah). In Hebrews (4:16; 7:19) the term is used metaphorically for the boldness the Christian has in prayer and for seeking forgiveness on the basis of Christ's already having done the work of purification.

Cultic washing was quite common in the Old Testament (cf. R. Meyer and F. Hauck, "*Katharos*," *TDNT*, vol. 3, pp. 421–25), but even there the cultic became a metaphorical symbol for moral purity: "Wash and make yourselves clean. Take your evil deeds out of my sight! Stop doing wrong, learn to do right!" (Isa. 1:16–17).

The **hands-hearts** combination is also found in the Old Testament: Pss. 24:4; 73:13.

Purify was used in both Old Testament and New Testament for cultic preparation to make one ready to worship (Num. 8:21; Josh. 3:5; 1 Chron. 15:2; John 11:55; Acts 21:24, 26). But Jesus speaks of the "pure in heart" as being blessed (Matt. 5:8) and means moral, not ritual, purity; cf. 1 Pet. 1:22 and 1 John 3:3.

Sinners are those who disobey God (Pss. 1:1–5; 51:15).

4:9 / Although the word **grieve** is not found elsewhere in the New Testament, a related word does occur in Rom. 3:16; 7:24; Rev. 3:17. Hermas *Similitudes* 1.3 uses "foolish and double-minded and miserable man," combining **double-minded** and miserable (**grieving**).

Mourning and **wail**ing are frequent in the Old Testament: Ps. 69:10–11; Isa. 32:11; Jer. 4:8; Amos 5:16; Mal. 3:14. Here there is anticipatory mourning in the face of judgment (cf. Amos 8:10).

Laughter and **joy** are associated with fools (Prov. 10:23; Sirach 21:20) and are marks of a profane life that lacks tension with the world. See further K. H. Rengstorf, "*Gelaō*," *TDNT*, vol. 1, pp. 658–61.

O. J. F. Seitz, "The Relationship of the Shepherd of Hermas to the Epistle of James," argues that James, 1 Clement 23:2–4, 2 Clement 11:2–3, and Hermas *Similitudes* 1.3 and *Visions* 3.7.1 all use the same lost apocryphal work. This is an interesting speculation, but Seitz does not prove that this must have been the case.

On mourning and wailing as signs of repentance see the literature on revivals, e.g., Jessie Penn-Lewis, *The Awakening in Wales* (Fort Washington, Penn.: Christian Literature Crusade, 1962) on the Welsh revival, or R. Lovelace, *The Dynamics of Spiritual Life* (Downers Grove, Ill.: Inter-Varsity Press, 1979), a more systematic treatment of revivals.

4:10 / On **lift up** see Job 5:11; 22:29; Ps. 149:4; Prov. 3:34; 29:25; Ezek. 17:24; 21:31. But Jesus' words are probably where James' ideas come from: Matt. 23:12; Luke 14:11; 18:14.

4:11 / The command **do not slander** can be read either with respect to slander or to criticism. In the Greek Old Testament the term at times means to speak falsely about a person (Lev. 19:16; Ps. 101:5; Prov. 20:13; Micah 3:7), but it also means unloving criticism or negative judgments, which may be true or false (Num. 12:8; 21:7; Ps. 77:19). In the intertestamental period, Testament of Issachar 3:4 connects the term with "censure," "being a busybody," and "envy." Paul rejects criticism as well: Rom. 1:30 points to it as pagan, while 2 Cor. 12:20 links it to whispering, gossip, or talebearing, as does 1 Pet. 2:12; 3:16. Later, 1 Clement 30:3 and 35:5 reject criticism, linking it to gossip and contrasting it to "clothing ourselves with harmony in humility." Hermas has a lot to say about slander (*Mandate* 8.3; *Similitude* 9.23.2–3), for example, the double-minded and slanderers are "never at peace among themselves, but always factious" (*Similitude* 8.7.2). "Defamation is evil; it is a restless demon, never at peace, but always dwells in dissension." Its opposite is simplicity (*Mandate* 2.1–3). See further S. S. Laws, *James*, pp. 186–87; W. Mundle, "Revile," *NIDNTT*, vol. 3, pp. 345–46.

The command not to judge is found repeatedly in the New Testament: Matt. 7:1–5; Luke 6:37–42; Rom. 2:1; 14:4; 1 Cor. 4:5; 5:12. The judging that is condemned does not include the proper use of the community disciplinary process (Matt. 18:15–20; 1 Cor. 5:1–5) or the proper use of *loving* criticism in private by elders and other Christians (e.g., Gal. 6:1ff.). See further M. Jeschke, *Disciplining the Brother* (Scottdale, Penn.: Herald Press, 1979), which is an excellent discussion of this issue.

4:12 / In the Greek Old Testament God is spoken of as the **Lawgiver** (Ps. 9:21 LXX [= Ps. 9:20 in Hebrew], "Appoint [yourself], O Lord, a lawgiver over them, / let the nations know that they are human beings."), as he is in the New Testament (Heb. 7:11 ["the law was given" by God]; 8:6 ["which is established in law upon better promises"]—in both these cases the NIV is far better English, but a wooden translation brings out the similar vocabulary). God's authority in judgment is frequently mentioned: Gen. 18:25; 1 Sam. 2:6; 1 Kings 5:7; Isa. 33:22; Matt. 10:28; Heb. 5:7. Hermas *Mandate* 12.6.3 refers to God as the one "who has all power, to save and to destroy." Thus James cites a much larger tradition that he does not have to prove.

§5 Praying for Endurance and Healing (James 4:13–5:20)

Throughout the book James has been dealing with the root causes of disharmony within the community. In the previous section, he has dealt with their complaining, their criticizing, and their roots in worldliness (3:1–4:12). Now he turns to another theme, the test of wealth. The poor person is totally dependent and knows it. Although such a person may well be consumed with envy and ambition, Christians are more likely to turn to prayer and humble dependence upon God. The wealthier person, however, may be lulled into a false sense of security and trust in money by the relative comfort of his or her station in life. It is this problem that James now takes up.

4:13 / Now listen shows that James is making a new departure in his thought. Those who should listen are a group of merchants making typical plans: **Today or tomorrow we will go to this or that city, spend a year there, carry on business and make money.** James does not call these people rich, for he reserves that term for unbelievers (2:6 and 5:1). These people are Christians, who may not be exactly wealthy, but are at least "middle-class."

The plans that these merchants are making do not seem ungodly. They are making travel plans (perhaps dependent upon when a ship or caravan is finally ready to leave). They have a destination in mind where they realize that their local goods (grain, wine, oil, or spices, if one thinks in terms of Palestine) can be profitably traded. They will **carry on business**, which means buy and sell goods. They expect the trading expedition to take a year, by which time their stock of goods to sell will be exhausted. They project a profit (**make money** does not indicate unusual amounts of profit). There appears to be nothing wrong. In trade a person has to plan ahead: Travel plans, market projections, time frames, and profit forecasts are the stuff of business in all ages. Every honest merchant would plan in exactly the same way—pagan, Jew, or Christian—and that is exactly the problem James has with these plans: There is absolutely nothing about their desires for the future, their use of money, or their way of doing business that is any different from the rest of the world. Their worship may be exemplary, their personal morality, impeccable; but when it comes to business they think entirely on a worldly plane.

4:14 / In contrast to the secure rationality of their plans stands the insecurity of life: **Why, you do not even know what will happen tomorrow.** In fact, life is utterly ephemeral: **You are a mist that appears for a little while and then vanishes.** Their projections are made; their plans are laid. But it all hinges on a will higher than theirs, a God unconsulted in their planning. That very night disease might strike; suddenly their plans evaporate, their only trip being one on a bier to a cold grave. They are like the rich fool of Jesus' parable, who had made a large honest profit through the chance occurrences of farming. Feeling secure, he makes rational plans for a comfortable retirement. "But God said to him, 'You fool! This very night your life will be demanded from you' " (Luke 12:16–21). By thinking on the worldly plane, James' Christian business people have gained a false sense of security. They need to look death in the face and realize their lack of control over life.

4:15 / Instead of relaxing in the false security of worldly thinking, they need to raise their thinking to a higher level: **If it is the Lord's will, we will live and do this or that.** This, of course, was precisely how Paul lived: Acts 18:21; Romans 1:10; 1 Corinthians 4:19; 16:7; Philippians 2:19, 24. The fact is that God alone controls whether we **live.** He alone controls whether we are able to **do this or that.** This acknowledgment recognizes human finiteness and divine sovereignty. But it does not rule out planning. The **we will** is a plan made in God's will.

This advice is not simply to add a "God willing" at the end of every plan. Rather, it is to plan with God. Each plan is evaluated by his standards and goals; each plan is laid before God in prayer with adequate time spent in *listening* for God's ideas. In such a case the "if God wills" is a prayerful belief that God *does* will, not a pious hope God won't interfere. Plans made with careful prayer and aimed at God's goals need not be insecure.

4:16 / These people, however, are far from *prayerful* planning: **As it is, you boast and brag. All such boasting is evil.** The key term is **boast**, for it indicates the inner attitude. Pride is the claim of the empty boaster, who claims an ability that he or she does not have. It is the claim of control and status in life that 1 John 2:16 cites, but the claim is false, for the world in the context of which the boast is made is passing away. It is "the presumptuous claims and ostentatious behavior of men by which they seek to impress one another, and very often delude themselves" (C. E. B. Cranfield, *The Epistle to the Romans* [Edinburgh, 1975], vol. 1, p. 132.) They **boast** in their empty plans of grandeur: "You should see the deal I'm going to get," or perhaps a more modest-sounding, "Well, tomorrow I'm going to Rome. My agent has lined up a fine shop right by the new agora. It is said only the wealthiest shop there." And on it goes: name-dropping, allusions to places and persons of power, gloating over deals to be made, but all of it empty boasting, for only God controls their lives. James evaluates this harshly: It is **evil**, for it robs God of his rightful honor as sovereign and exalts a mere human as if he or she were God. Any plan confidently made outside God's will discerned through prayer and meditation is not just foolish—it is sin.

4:17 / To round off his thought, James adds a concluding proverb, which some speculate might be a saying of Jesus because of its tone and topic: **Anyone, then, who knows the good he ought to do and doesn't do it, sins.** On the surface it simply rebukes sins of omission: A person who knows he or she should do something (e.g., give to a poor person) but neglects to do it has not just missed an opportunity for obedience—he or she has sinned. The context, however, lifts this out of the arena of general truth and into the lives of these merchants. There is clearly something they **know** they **ought to do** and are thus responsible for (Luke 12:47–48), which is to obey and follow God in business. But their business interests often lead them to worldly planning and hoarding like the rich fool (Luke 12:13–21). To do **the good** in scripture is frequently to do charitable acts (James 1:21–25 and Gal. 6:9). James, then, may be suggesting that they plan like the world because they are motivated by the world, for God has his own way to invest money: give it to the poor (Matt. 6:19–21). If they took God into account they might not be trying to increase their own standard of living; God might lead them to relieve the suffering around them, that is, to do good.

Having spoken to Christians whose hearts were being seduced by the world, James now turns to address wealthy non-Christians. He roundly condemns them in language similar to Jesus' (Luke 6:20–26), in order to turn Christians away from the seductiveness of wealth and to prepare them to endure the test of suffering at the hands of the wealthy.

5:1 / Now listen, you rich people. In calling these people **rich** he classes them with the non-Christians he cites in 2:6 and 1:9. These people, unlike those addressed in 4:14, are outside the Christian fold, so there will be no comforting words for them. There may be forgiveness if they turn from their ways, repent, and join the community of Christians, but James expresses no hope this will happen. His intention is to encourage the Christian community, not to convert the rich.

The call is to **weep and wail because of the misery that is coming upon you**. Just as the poor Christian is to rejoice in present suffering (1:2, 12), so this anticipated joy is matched by anticipated sorrow for the rich. In the middle of their wealth and luxury they should wail, crying out in deep sorrow as if in response to death or disaster (e.g., Isa. 15:1–6). James fully realizes that they are not *presently* suffering, so he says, **is coming upon you**. They have plenty to eat, reasonable economic security, social status, and power. But like Isaiah (Isa. 13:6), James looks with divine foresight and sees the dark hurricane cloud of the Day of the Lord about to strike them down.

5:2–3 / The initial warning leads to a vivid description of their misery seen through prophetic eyes. **Your wealth has rotted** is a general description of their state: All their security, all that their hopes and dreams are built upon, has already rotted, from James' eternal perspective. This is made specific by naming the two classes of wealth that were commonly saved. First, **moths have eaten your clothes**. They have had closets full of clothing, which might have been used by the poor, but before they look worn the moths get to them. Today one might as easily say, "Your clothes are hopelessly out of style." Second, **your gold and silver are corroded**. They have stored their wealth, but it helps neither them nor the poor, for it is saved for "a rainy day." Its very tarnish shows it is not needed. Today, when money is stored in banks, one might say, "Your money is devalued by inflation." James' teaching is therefore similar to that of Jesus: "Do not store up for yourselves treasures on earth, where moth and rust destroy, and where thieves break in and steal. But store up for yourselves treasures in heaven, where moth and rust do not destroy, and where thieves to not break in and steal. For where your treasure is, there your heart will be also" (Matt. 6:19–21).

This stored wealth has a consequence, for **their corrosion will testify against you and eat your flesh like fire**. The image is that of the final judgment, as if the tarnished coins and the moth-eaten garments were displayed before the court. The evidence condemns them, for if God had been served, the stored goods would have been used to clothe the naked and feed the hungry. Like the rich man in the parable (Luke 16:19–31), they are flung into hell, "where the fire never goes out" (Mark 9:43). James pictures this as if the very tarnish that ate into their silver now eats into them like fire, perhaps picturing the inward torment of guilt at the wasted treasure that forever condemns them.

In a sense the day of judgment is already present: **You have hoarded wealth in the last days**. James is convinced that in the coming of Jesus time has been totally altered, for he announced, "the kingdom of God is near" (e.g., Mark 1:15), which indicated that the old age was ending and the new beginning, inaugurating the last days. When the Spirit came at Pentecost, Peter saw it as a sign of the last days, "In the last days, God says, I will pour out my Spirit on all people" (Acts 2:17, as also 2 Tim. 3:1; Heb.

1:2). The end is not a distant future point for the church, for it itself lives in the new life of the coming age, as it serves its king. In this context, the piling up of riches is tragically ironic. The rich gather and invest as if they or their descendants will live forever, yet the last days, the beginning of the end, are already here. James sees as tragic figures well-dressed men and women pondering investments over excellent meals; they act as if they were winners, but in reality have lost the only game that matters.

5:4 / Furthermore, James knows accumulated wealth usually indicates injustice, which in Palestine was usually injustice against agricultural workers. **Look! The wages you failed to pay the workmen who mowed your fields are crying out against you.** The Palestinian economy used hired day laborers rather than slaves, partly because a slave would cost more should he or she convert to Judaism. The hired laborers would be the younger sons of peasant families or peasants forced off their land due to the foreclosure of mortgages on their property. These laborers lived a hand-to-mouth existence: Today's wage bought tomorrow's breakfast. When the wage was not paid at the end of the day, the whole family went hungry. Despite a host of Old Testament laws (Lev. 19:13; Deut. 24:14–15), ways were found to withhold payment (e.g., Jer. 22:13; Mal. 3:5). One might withhold them until the end of the harvest season to keep the worker coming back, appeal to a technicality to show that the contract was not fulfilled, or just be too tired to pay that night. If the poor worker complained, the landlord could blacklist him; if he went to court the rich had the better lawyers. James pictures the money in the pockets of the rich, money that should have been paid to the laborers, crying out for justice.

The cries have not gone unheard, for **the cries of the harvesters have reached the ears of the Lord Almighty.** Since they are **harvesters,** there is no excuse that there was no money; there are heaps of grain to be sold. The hungry worker has cried out to the only resource he has—God. By saying **the Lord Almighty,** James reminds the reader of Isaiah 5:9, where those acquiring large estates are condemned. All Jews knew what happened to those whom Isaiah condemned, and they knew that God's ears are open to the poor (Pss. 17:1–6; 18:6; 31:2), so James' statement implies a threat of judgment.

5:5 / The rich live in contrast to the suffering of the poor: **You have lived on earth in luxury and self-indulgence**. Many of the rich might have protested that they were simply middle-class and had earned their few pleasures. James looks at them from the perspective of the poor and calls it indulgence, which 1 Timothy 5:6 sees as a vice. And it is indeed indulgence in the face of the suffering of others. To this James adds, **You have fattened yourselves in the day of slaughter**. The Greek has two meanings. On the one hand, it means: "You have enjoyed yourselves on the day of slaughter." Since the fresh meat was soon dried or salted, it was customary to have a big barbecue when one slaughtered animals. But on the other hand, James understands the double meaning, which the NIV correctly expresses. The wealthy have plenty to eat; they enjoy life. But it is the biblical day of slaughter, the day God slaughters his enemies (e.g., Isa. 30:33; 34:5–8). They have enjoyed life as if on a day of slaughter, yet ironically *they* are now the fattened calf and God's slaughter knife is about to fall.

5:6 / To emphasize their impending doom, James adds a final charge: **You have condemned and murdered innocent [people], who were not opposing you**. The first part of the charge is familiar, for it is a charge of judicial murder, either by active or passive means. Actively the courts are used to have inconvenient righteous people executed. Passively the courts are used to rob the poor of their livelihood by taking their farms or other means of support. It is all "perfectly legal," and the poor "just happen" to die of diseases related to malnutrition. God calls both types murder.

The last half of the charge is more difficult. It is true that the poor often cannot resist the rich and powerful and so frequently hardly protest. Furthermore, the tradition of the gospel is nonresistance to evil (Matt. 5:39), and this nonresistance might be seen as a sign of the new age and thus of coming doom. But the tone of the passage demands a question: "Do they not resist you?" On earth the poor appear not to resist: The rich do not hear the groaning cry in prayer before the poor person dies. But James knows that that is not the end: In heaven the wronged continue to raise their cry, "How long?" (Rev. 6:9–11), for they have an audience in the very presence of God. This is indeed effective resistance, for God will hear.

James has finished his argument. All that remains for him is to summarize (5:7-11) and to add a proper epistolary conclusion (5:12-20: oaths, health wish, purpose). Here his pastoral heart comes out as he advises the community how to live during these "last days."

5:7 / **Be patient** is his first advice. Here patience means "enduring," "keeping steady under provocation." It is the same as "the ability to endure" of 1:2 or "remains faithful" of 1:12. The answer to unfaithfulness in the community or persecution from without is not to strike back but to continue to be faithful. The life of discipleship is its own witness. Just as patience/endurance (i.e., neither compromise nor confrontation), it is a big demand.

Patience lasts **until the Lord's coming**. This does not mean that one should make no efforts to ameliorate conditions beforehand: a faithful witness will help conditions in the world as a demonstration of the new life in Christ, but the hope of the Christian is in the second coming. The world will not be destroyed or evil defeated until Christ returns personally to destroy it, root and branch.

Patience is never easy, especially if one is suffering. To bolster their hopes James uses the example of **the farmer**. For the Palestinian farmer, the crops were literally his life and were therefore **valuable**. His energy had gone into plowing, weeding, and chasing birds away. He had sowed seed his family might otherwise have eaten. He had waited patiently for the **autumn**, or early, **rains** (October-November) before sowing. After the sowing he waited for the **spring**, or later, **rains** (March-April) to ripen the crop. All this time his food supplies were getting lower; it was not uncommon for food to be rationed and the children to be crying from hunger during the month or two before harvest. The later the rains, the worse it was. But with his life in his hands he had to wait for conditions outside his control.

5:8 / Christians also must **be patient**. Like the farmer, the Christian bets his or her life on the outcome of a long wait. Like the farmer, reducing the tension (by compromise or attack) would be self-destructive. The Christian must place all hope in a condition outside his or her control, waiting patiently for the coming of the King.

As they wait they are to **stand firm.** As they wait doubt must
be fought at all costs: The inner defenses must be constantly at-
tended, their hearts must be strengthened in the face of suffering.

As a further encouragement he adds, **the Lord's coming
is near.** For the rich this is bad news (5:3–5); for believers this is
good news. The waiting may still be long, but like a runner who
has rounded the last curve on the track and sees the finish line
down the interminable straightaway, they can receive a new wind
from the vision of the end.

5:9 / Having summarized Christian patience as a response to testing, James now summarizes his teaching on speech,
commanding, **Don't grumble against each other.** The term
grumble is "to groan." A groan might be an appropriate response
to suffering (Mark 7:34), but the operant word is **against each
other.** Here the sigh is a complaint against a community member, an overt criticism (4:11), or an eloquent sigh that invites a
question, and then a reluctant "since you asked" explanation.
However expressed, criticism is a great temptation in a community under pressure, both in terms of displaced hostility or jealousy (because someone has life easier than you). James realized
that this was destructive to the community, the solidarity of which
was vital to support the Christians during hard times. The reason not to complain is **or you will be judged,** which draws on
the teaching of Jesus: "Do not judge, or you too will be judged.
For in the same way you judge others, you will be judged" (Matt.
7:1–2). God will be as harsh on the believer as the believer is harsh
on others, and a person can never endure his own criticism, for
people frequently criticize their own weaknesses in others. James
goes beyond Jesus in arguing that since God in Jesus commands
the believer not to judge, the very act of criticizing or complaining is disobedience.

Furthermore James adds: **The Judge is standing at the door!**
The picture is that of Christ standing before a door of the house
church, his hand reaching out to lift the latch and open it. This
is no time to be caught criticizing one another. Like children in
a schoolroom hearing the hoarse whisper "the teacher's coming,"
so the Christians should quiet down. The nearness of Christ's
coming both warns and encourages.

5:10 / With the theme of speech summarized, James moves to that of suffering: **Take the prophets who spoke in the name of the Lord.** By **the prophets** James includes more than just the writing prophets, but all the worthies, obscure and well known, cited in Jewish martyrologies, as well as in Hebrews 11. By using the phrase **who spoke in the name of the Lord**, he both excludes false prophets and focuses on the true prophets' crucial characteristic: They confessed true faith in God by word and deed. There is no need to cite them by name, for Jewish Christians had learned the stories.

The prophets are to be looked at **as an example of patience in the face of suffering.** Their crucial virtue was the ability to endure, whatever the trials. Whether an Amos commanded not to speak (Amos 7) or an Elijah pursued by Jezebel (1 Kings 19:1ff.) or a Jeremiah imprisoned by King Zedekiah (Jer. 38), these people endured. Reflection on them yields two facts: (1) the lot of a servant of God often involves suffering, and (2) a person can endure the suffering and remain faithful.

5:11 / In their own day prophets were regarded as reactionary fossils who did not like the modern trends in worship. They were seen as dangerous visionaries who believed that God, not strategic alliances, would protect the nation. Some were even thought to be weak-kneed traitors who suggested surrender (e.g., Jeremiah). Many people probably said, "I admire his convictions, but he seems to be rather masochistic, virtually demanding martyrdom by going public." Others were glad when the prophet was dead and gone. The suffering itself was far from glamorous, with no angel choirs lending a glow to the setting. Yet now **we consider blessed those who have persevered.** Matthew 5:11–12 is the background, for Jesus calls blessed those suffering for good deeds. This is a reversal of the world's evaluation, and James implies that "the same happiness can be yours." Since the prophets' happiness was because they did not give up but **persevered**, perseverance is also required of Christians. In this vein, Jesus had earlier said that the truly saved is "whoever holds out to the end" (Matt. 10:22; 24:13; Luke 21:19), and Paul will point out that it is those who cross the finish line who gain the prize (1 Cor. 9:24–27; Phil. 3:13–14; cf. 2 Tim. 4:6–8).

As a concrete prophet James cites Job: **You have heard of Job's perseverance, and have seen what the Lord finally brought about**. The story of Job was a favorite in Jewish circles; he is cited as early as Ezekiel 14:14, 29. By the time of James, many embellished versions existed that enlarged upon the canonical account in two directions: (1) they emphasized Job's endurance under testing, and (2) they stressed his righteousness, especially his great charity. The important point for James, however, is that as much as Job complained, he refused to give up his trust or to disobey God, and **the Lord finally brought about** his deliverance. The call to the Christian, then, is not to give up and to lose the reward *now*, after all that has already been endured, but to keep holding on.

Driving his point home, James adds a single clause: **The Lord is full of compassion and mercy**. James is citing Ps. 103:8 or 111:4 (probably from memory), and the quotation is most appropriate. God does not like watching people squirm. He would not allow suffering to happen if there were not a far greater good ahead. On this note the summary ends: Trust God and keep on patiently enduring, for the Lord is unimaginably concerned about you.

5:12 / James is ready to end his letter, so he puts in his equivalents of the customary endings of a Greek literary letter. The first part of such an ending was frequently an oath to guarantee its truth, so having first used a common ending formula (**above all**), James takes up the topic: **Do not swear**. Although the Old Testament regulated oaths and demanded that if one used an oath one must fulfill the promise (e.g., Exod. 20:7), it did not prohibit oaths (cf. Exod. 22:10–11). Throughout the Old Testament period there are a series of warnings against using oaths too lightly (e.g., Jer. 5:2), and later Sirach advised not using oaths, so one would not frivolously use one (23:9, 11). Jesus, however, prohibited all oaths, using the words **Do not swear—not by heaven or by earth** (the **or by anything else** in James summarizes the rest of Jesus' saying in Matt. 5:34–37). James has picked up and summarized the words of Jesus; the readers would recognize the source.

Christians are not to use oaths. Among the common oaths of the day were **by heaven** or **by earth**. None are to be used: **Let** your "Yes" be yes, and your "No," no. If one resorted to oaths it divided speech into two categories: promises one really meant (guaranteed by an oath) and promises that could not be trusted. The Christian demand is for absolute faithfulness and truthfulness in all speech. There should be no social hypocrisy in which one says something other than what is in the heart. This demand is important, for not to observe it means **you will be condemned**. God is the guarantor of *all* speech. He will judge every word. God's judgment is the standard Christians should fear and observe.

5:13 / The second topic of a closing in a Greek letter was health; James pursues it extensively, setting the topic within the context of verbal responses to life. First, **is anyone of you in trouble? He should pray.** The **trouble** James refers to is the misfortunes of life: persecutions, like those the prophets suffered (5:10; cf. 5:1–6); external misfortunes, like Job suffered (5:11); or being slandered by a community member (3:1–12; cf. 2:6–7). All of these are external misfortunes, which one could easily see as outside of God's will, for they stem from the evil in the world and are attacks upon the righteous. The response to such evil is not counterattack (fighting violence with violence) or resignation (as the Stoics advised) but prayer. The psalmist appealed to God to deal with his persecutors (Pss. 30; 50:15; 91:15), and this is also the Christian response.

Second, **is anyone happy? Let him sing songs of praise**. Too often happiness or joy is taken for granted. James reminds Christians that there is a proper use of the tongue in joy as well, for the New Testament constantly commands Christians to be full of the praise of God, at home or at work, as well as in Church (e.g., 1 Cor. 14:15; Eph. 5:19; Col. 3:16; Phil. 4:4).

5:14 / Third, **is any one of you sick?** Illness was a far more difficult situation than external suffering. War, persecution, or ostracism can be blamed on human evil, but illness appears outside the human sphere and thus invites the question, "Why did this happen to me?" Or, more pointedly, "What have I done to deserve this?" And the New Testament treats illness using different terminology and a different response than that reserved for suffering (which always means that which one experiences because one is a Christian).

In line with the general New Testament attitude, James responds to the issue of illness quite differently to his response to suffering: **He should call the elders of the church to pray over him and anoint him with oil in the name of the Lord**. This means that prayer again is the response to suffering, but in this case the counseling and prayers of the leaders of the church are involved. The local church was run by a council of elders; some of them would come to the person when requested. It is interesting that the **elders** are called, not people with a specific gift of healing (as in 1 Cor. 12:9, 28, 30), although healing gifts were not a requirement for selection as elders. Apparently James felt that because of the relationship of healing to pastoral ministry (cf 5:15), the elders as a body should be involved and were gifted for the task by reason of their office.

When the elders respond, they do two things. First, they pray for the person. This is the activity that receives the stress by being put first. They call upon God to heal the person; they do not heal by their own virtue. Second, they **anoint** the person **with oil** in the name of the Lord. Though oil was often used as a medicine (Luke 10:34), this is not presented as a medicinal treatment. Rather, it is an outward and physically perceptible sign of the spiritual power of prayer, as well as a sign of the authority of the healer (Mark 6:13). It corresponds to healing prayer as water does to baptismal prayer. It is done **in the name of the Lord**, for as in baptism (Acts 2:38), the name of Jesus is invoked in prayer as the power and authority of the act.

5:15 / This action will be effective, for the **prayer offered in faith will make the sick person well**. **Prayer** is the term that covers all of the preceding. Although there was oil and probably laying on of hands, it is not the physical actions that possess potency but the prayer to God, which they physically act out. This prayer is **offered in faith**: The uttering of even the best and finest prayer is no guarantee of assistance if it does not come from the heart. James had already pointed out that trust in God and obedience to his commands is essential to prayer (1:5–8; 4:1–3), now he applies the teaching. Without the life of commitment to

God that the prayer *expresses*, it will be ineffectual. The faith lies in the elders, not in the sick person (about whose faith nothing is said). The elders' faith is critical: If something "goes wrong" it is they, not the sick person, who bear the onus.

The promise is **the Lord will raise him up**. In Greek it is clearly physical healing, not just spiritual preparation for death, that James is concerned with, and it is the Lord's action that does the healing, not the oil, the hands, or the power of the elders. The Lord remains sovereign: God answers prayer; he is not compelled by prayer.

Finally, **If he has sinned, he will be forgiven**. Sin may well be the underlying reason for the illness, but it is not necessarily the cause. Apparently an opportunity for confession of sins was offered by the elders (this counseling aspect may be why *elders* in particular were called). The confession was raised to God along with the disease, and the resulting healing confirms that God has forgiven the person. But although such a process should be offered, if no sin is known, that is fine. James' "**If**" is an important word, and to push beyond it to *demand* confession is to violate scripture and pastoral wisdom.

5:16 / James summarizes his teaching on healing in two sentences. First, **confess your sins to each other and pray for each other so that you may be healed**. Confession of sin is important for healing. Pastors experienced in the Christian healing ministry repeatedly witness to times when the confession of a resentment, a grudge, or an unforgiven injury has lead to physical healing with or without further prayer. But James is generalizing beyond the individual healing situation, for now it is not "to the elders" but **to each other** that confession is made. The picture is that of a church gathering and the confession of sin to the assembled group. The mutual public confession (supplemented by private confession where public confession would not be appropriate) lays the basis for public prayer, in which people freed from all grudges and resentments, and reconciled through confession and forgiveness, pray for healing for each other. In this kind of atmosphere, the services of the elders at the bedside will rarely be needed.

Second, **the prayer of a righteous [person] is powerful and effective**. The **righteous** person is not sinlessly perfect, but is the

person who has confessed any known sin and who adheres to
the moral standards of the Christian community. With a clear conscience and in unity with God, this person prays a prayer that
is powerful and effective. The Greek adds a difficult expression
that probably means "when it reaches God and he answers it"
(lit. "when it works"). Prayer is not *itself* powerful; it is not magic.
But its power is unlimited in that the child of God calls on a Father
of unlimited goodness and ability.

5:17–18 / To back up his assertion of the power of prayer,
James cites **Elijah** (1 Kings 17:1–18:46). Though the Old Testament says very little about it, later Jewish tradition focused on
Elijah's prayer. James cites the length of the drought to underline
the power of the prayer. Moreover, the prayer was not just destructive but also healing, for he prayed and the drought promptly
ended (much more important for the Christians James is addressing, who presumably are interested in healing and thus will be
more encouraged by prayer's causing rain to fall and grass to grow
than by its causing a drought).

Furthermore, **Elijah was a [person] just like us**. In Jewish
tradition, as in the Old Testament, Elijah is very human. He is
godly, but often falls prey to doubts and depression. Elijah does
not stride across the stage of history ten feet tall but as an or-
dinary man with an extraordinary God. Since he is **like us**, any
Christian, as a person obedient to God, has the same power. The
mission may be different, but if simple prayer was enough for
Elijah's great mission, it will surely suffice for that of any believer.

5:19 / Finally, James is ready to end the letter, but as he
does he follows the customary procedure of stating his purpose.
Addressing the believers (**my brothers**), he proposes to them a
situation: **if one of you should wander from the truth and someone should bring him back**. To speak of wandering is to speak
of a serious departure from the true faith, such as idolatry (e.g.,
Isa. 9:16). The Christian life can be described as a way of life opposed to the way of death; to wander from the way of life is to
stumble onto the broad road to hell (Matt. 7:13–14). The ways of
life and death do not cross, for as James has argued (4:4), the
world and God are mutually exclusive. The picture brings John
Bunyan's *Pilgrim's Progress* to mind.

The truth is not intellectual facts but a way of life. James is not concerned about doctrinal error, the dotting of eschatological i's or the crossing of ecclesiological t's, but about one central truth: Jesus is Lord! The whole of the book has been demonstrating what this Lordship means in the concrete life of the people. If Jesus is not obeyed, one has lost the central truth and become entangled in a morass of sin and death.

If a person wanders away, the rest of the community is not just to let him or her go, but to try to **bring him back**. As Paul (Gal. 6:1) and John (1 John 5:16-17) also taught, the goal is not judgment but restoration. Yet restoration and forgiveness cannot come without repentance (cf. Luke 17:3-4). So the first task is not to "accept" someone as he or she sinks, but to reach out to the person, turn the person, and get him or her back on the path.

5:20 / This task of bringing the sinner to repentance will not be without its rewards: **Whoever turns a sinner from the error of his way will save him from death and cover over a multitude of sins**. James recognizes that the person who has left the truth is a **sinner**, whose **way** is in **error**. The Didache begins, "There are two ways—one of life, and one of death. And there is a great difference between the two ways" (1:1). This sober fact is fundamental, for it comes from Jesus (especially the Sermon on the Mount). Where the distinction between the ways is blurred, no rescue effort can begin.

Furthermore, the sinner's soul is in danger of **death**. Though James might mean physical death, which he knows can result from sin (5:14-16; 1 Cor. 11:30), it is far more likely he means spiritual and eternal death (Jude 22-23). James recognizes the seriousness of the person's situation, and this conviction drives him to a rescue effort. He has written 108 verses to try to rescue some from what he knows is death.

But the story does not end there. The wanderer has been brought back again. God does not desire the sinner's death, but his or her repentance. God's grace is still available no matter how much he has been wronged (4:6). The sinner, then, is delivered from death. The jaws of hell snap shut on air as the believer once again walks the way of life. The rescue has resulted in the forgiveness **of a multitude of sins**, which are **covered over**, forgotten.

The person is not branded in the church as someone who once went astray but is part of a company in which all are forgiven sinners. This is James' goal in writing. He points out the wrong way in hope that the people will turn back and their sins will be forgotten forever. With this note of grace and forgiveness he ends his work.

Additional Notes §5

4:13 / In Greek the **now listen** is exactly parallel to the "Now listen" of 5:1, which shows that the two passages fit together.

The merchants were upwardly mobile in Palestine. In that day the oldest son took over the property of his father and younger sons were given money and told to make their own fortune. Trade was the best way to make money. It entailed risk, but it was the only way to get ahead, for small farming was too uncertain and the large population of Palestine put pressure on the land, keeping prices up and interest fairly high. So one took a large stock of goods to a place they were scarce and attempted to trade at a profit for the rare goods of that land (e.g., Matt. 13:45–46). When all had been sold, one took the foreign goods back to Palestine and sold them at a profit. The ideal was to repeat the cycle until one was able to buy a large estate and become part of the landed gentry, who had the highest social status. See further S. W. Baron, *A Social and Religious History of the Jews*, vol. 1, pp. 255–59; F. C. Grant, *The Economic Background of the Gospels*, pp. 72–76. and J. Jeremias, *Jerusalem in the Time of Jesus*, pp. 30–57, 195.

4:14 / The idea that life is like a **mist** was common in the ancient world. The Old Testament uses the image frequently (Job 7:7, 9, 16; Ps. 39:5–6; Prov. 27:1; Eccles. 8:7), as did the intertestamental wisdom tradition (Sirach 11:18–19; Wisdom 2:1–2; 3:14); 1 Clement quotes a similar saying (17:6). Though the teaching of Jesus might be the immediate basis of this teaching, it draws on a widespread biblical background.

4:15 / Many Greek and Jewish writers knew the wisdom of **if it is the Lord's will**. The late first-century rabbi Jose said, "Let all thy actions be to the Name of Heaven" (m. *Aboth* 2:16, cf. 2:14). A confession of this truth occurs in a Dead Sea Scroll (1 QS 11:10–11). Ignatius said the same years later (To the Ephesians 10:1). See further G. Schrenk, *"Thelō," TDNT*, vol. 3, p. 47.

4:16 / The term **boast** is rarely used in the New Testament in this form (only in 1 John 2:16), although the same phrase, **proud and**

you boast or boast in your pride, is found in 1 Clement 21:5. Yet a related word for pride appears in two New Testament vice lists (Rom. 1:30 and 2 Tim. 3:2) as well as in the Greek Old Testament (Job 28:2; Prov. 21:24; 2 Macc. 9:8). It is always a vice, never a virtue; it is closely related to boasting in all New Testament contexts, as pride and conceit normally are related. John makes it a characteristic of the world (1 John 2:16). In secular Greek the emptiness of the boast becomes clear, for it designates primarily the person who claims an ability or virtue he or she does not have. See further G. Delling, *"Alazon," TDNT,* vol. 1, pp. 226–27; and E. Gutting and C. Brown, "Pride," *NIDNTT,* vol. 3, pp. 28–32.

Boasting is rarely virtuous. One may boast legitimately in God, in suffering and humiliation, or in service (Rom. 5:2–3; 1 Cor 13:3b; Phil. 2:16; 1 Thess. 2:9; cf. 1 Clement 21:5), but most boasting is an evil self-sufficiency (Rom 3:27; 4:2; 1 Cor. 1:20; 5:6; Gal. 6:13–14). See also the comment on James 3:14.

4:17 / The teaching about not doing **good** that it is possible to do is also in the Old Testament (e.g., Job 31:16–20) and is based on teachings such as Deut. 15:7–11. It is the basis of the parable of the rich man and Lazarus (Luke 16:19–31), for the rich man is condemned to hell simply because there was a need at his gate that he could have met but did not; he should have known better from the Old Testament.

The ability of business to distract a person from proper devotion was proverbial in James' day: Sirach 11:10; 31:5–11 ("he who pursues money will be led astray by it"). That may be why Agur asks for neither *poverty* nor *wealth* (Prov. 30:7–9).

5:1 / In addressing **you rich people** James goes beyond the warnings of Wisdom 2 and Hermas *Vision* 3.9.3–6, which both see the danger of wealth, and reaches the "how terrible for you who are rich now" of Jesus (Luke 6:24) and the "woe to you, you rich, for you have trusted in your riches, and from your riches shall you depart," of 1 Enoch 94:8 (cf. 94:6–97:10). For James, as for Jesus, hoarded wealth is evil.

Weep in the Old Testament comes in the face of disaster (Lam. 1:1–2; Jer. 9:1; 13:17) The term **wail** is not found elsewhere in the New Testament but is frequent in Old Testament prophets (e.g., Isa. 10:1; 14:31; Jer. 31:20, 31; Ezek. 21:12; Hos. 7:14; Amos 8:3). See further H. W. Heidland, *"Ololyzō," TDNT,* vol. 5, pp. 173–74.

Misery is another prophetic term, used elsewhere in the New Testament in Rom. 3:16 (quoting Isa. 59:7; cf. Isa. 47:11; Jer. 6:7, 26). A related term appears in James 4:9. Like Amos (6:1–9) or Jesus (Matt 8:12; 13:42; 19:24), James sees beyond the present comfortable state of the rich and calls for mourning in the face of impending misery.

5:2–3 / The images in these verses are traditional in the intertestamental tradition. "To rot" is found in Sirach 14:19 and Baruch 6:72; **moths have eaten** occurs in Job 13:28; Prov. 25:20; Isa. 33:1; 50:9; Sirach 42:13; and **corroded** occurs in Sirach 12:11; 29:10; Baruch 6:12, 24. James knew gold and silver did not rust, but they would build up heavy tarnish. So the analogy was used, in the tradition, for stored and useless money: "Help a poor man for the commandment's sake. . . . Lose your silver for the sake of a brother or a friend, and do not let it rust under a stone and be lost. Lay up your treasure according to the commandment of the Most High [i.e., give it away in charity] and it will profit you more than gold. Store up almsgiving in your treasure, and it will rescue you from all affliction" (Sirach 29:8–13; cf. Matt. 6:19–21 and Luke 12:13–34). James applies Jesus' teaching about the rich man in Luke 16: The stored wealth is not just lost; it will condemn the person to hell. See further, P. H. Davids, "The New Testament Foundation for Living More Simply," in *Living More Simply*, R. Sider, ed., (Downers Grove, Ill.: Inter-Varsity Press, 1980).

The connection of **eat your flesh like fire** with final judgment is made in Judith 16:17: "The Lord Almighty will take vengeance on them in the day of judgment; fire and worms he will give to their flesh; they shall weep in pain for ever"; cf. Num. 12:12; Isa. 30:27; Ezek. 7:19; 15:7; Amos 1:12; 5:6; Wisdom 1:18; Acts 11:5. The **flesh** means the whole person (Lev. 26:29; Job 4:15). **Fire**, as a metaphor for hell, comes from the teaching of Jesus (e.g., Matt. 25:41) and later apocalyptic works (2 Pet. 3:7; Jude 23; Rev. 11:5; 20:9). See H. Bietenhard, "Fire," *NIDNTT*, vol. 1, pp. 652–58; and "Hell," *NIDNTT*, vol. 2, pp. 205–10.

The **last days**, meaning judgment and the day of God's action, is drawn from the Old Testament: Isa. 2:2; Jer. 23:20; Ezek. 38:16; Dan. 2:28; Hos. 3:5. This idea is foundational to the tension in James, for whom the judge is "at the door" (5:8–9). See further S. S. Laws, *James*, pp. 198–99; O. Cullmann, *Christ and Time*; or G. E. Ladd, *The Presence of the Future* (Grand Rapids: Wm. B. Eerdmans, 1974) or *A Theology of the New Testament* (Grand Rapids: Wm. B. Eerdmans), pp. 57–80, 91–119, 193–212.

5:4 / The **workmen who mowed your fields** also appear in Jesus' parables (Matt. 9:37; 10:10; Mark 1:20; Luke 10:2; 15:17). In the Old Testament righteous people might protest that they always paid their workers on time (Job 7:1–2; 24:10; 31:13, 38–40).

The **cries** are cries for justice (Gen. 4:10; Exod. 2:20; 1 Sam. 9:16; Ps. 12:5; Rev. 6:9–10; Hermas *Vision* 3.9.6).

The **Lord Almighty** is a term characteristic of Isaiah, who uses it sixty-one times, versus nine times in the rest of the Old Testament.

The charge of withholding wages may be intended literally, or it may stand as a typical example of a class of abuses, including building large estates (Isa. 5:7–9; Mark 12:40; Luke 20:47).

5:5 / **Luxury and self-indulgence** are condemned throughout scripture (Ezek. 16:49; Amos 2:6–8; 8:4–6; Luke 16:19–31). James uses the same word Jesus used to describe the lifestyle of the rich man in Luke 16 (cf. 1 Enoch 98:11; 102:9–10; Hermas *Similitude* 6.1.6; 6.2.6; Barnabas 10.3).

On **fattened yourselves** as an image of indulging pleasures, see Isa. 6:10; Ps. 104:15; Mark 7:21; Luke 21:34; and T. Sorg, "Heart," *NIDNTT,* vol. 2, p. 182.

The **day of slaughter** occurs in Jer. 46:10; 50:26–27; Ezek. 39:17; Pss. 22:29; 37:20; 49:14; Rev. 19:17–21. In 1 Enoch the judgment on the rich is described, "Ye . . . have become ready for the day of slaughter, and the day of darkness and the day of the great judgment" (1 Enoch 94:9; cf. 97:8–10; 99:15; Jubilees 36:9–10). The Dead Sea Scrolls speak of it as "the day of massacre" (1 QH 15:17–18).

5:6 / The concept of judicial condemnation (**condemned and murdered**) is frequent in the Old Testament: Pss. 10:8–9; 37:14, 32; Prov. 1:11–14; Isa. 3:13–15; 57:1; Amos 2:6; 5:12. Wisdom 2:20, "Let us condemn [the righteous] to a shameful death, for according to what he says, he will be protected," has been seen by some commentators as the source of this verse in James. The theme is close to James, but there are no verbal parallels to prove literary dependence. Much of the tradition sounds as if murder of the poor were involved. Many of these passages are poetic (e.g., Ps. 10) and may give God's view of a matter that the people saw differently. Some poor suffered like Naboth (1 Kings 21), but far more suffered from legal confiscation of goods (as in Isa. 3), which only God saw as unjust and immoral. This was frequently termed "murder" in Jewish tradition (e.g., Sirach 34:21–22: "the bread of the needy is the life of the poor; whoever deprives them of it is a man of blood. To take away a neighbor's living is to murder him; to deprive an employee of his wages is to shed blood.")

The term **innocent** [people] is actually singular. The NIV correctly reads it as a collective noun, but because of its singular form, some few commentators have felt it referred to a specific righteous person, either Jesus (as in Acts 3:14; 7:52; 22:14) or James (called "the Just" or "the righteous" in Eusebius' *Ecclesiastical History* 2.23). But the strength of the Old Testament parallels is so strong that it is far more probable that the reference is to the suffering Christian poor viewed generically. See further S. S. Laws, *James,* pp. 204–6.

The **who were not opposing you** again has a "he" (singular), not a "they" (plural). The NIV reads it as a collective. As an alternative it has "Will God [i.e., he] not resist you?" Others have suggested, "Did [or does] he [i.e., Christ] resist you?" Whereas this commentary suggests "Do they not resist you?" The problem is that the "he" is ambiguous and in Greek only context can differentiate a question from a statement. There is a strong teaching of nonresistance in scripture (Isa. 53:7; Matt. 5:39; Rom. 12:19; 1 Pet. 2:23; cf. Hermas *Mandate* 8.10, where "resist no one" is a "good thing" pointing to salvation), which led to the pacifist tradition of the early church (see J. M. Hornus, *It Is Not Lawful for Me to Fight* [Scottdale, Penn.: Herald Press, 1980]). Yet though James clearly does not expect the Christians to resist (cf. 5:7) but to suffer patiently (itself a warning that the new age had dawned), given the Rev. 6 passage and the lack of a clear interpretation of nonresistance in James, it is more likely that heavenly resistance is in mind.

5:7 / Although a different word for **patient** is used here than in 1:2, 12 (*makrothymē* vs. *hypomonē*), the two terms are used in parallel in Col. 1:11. Thus, as in 4:1–3 vs. 1:13–15 there is variety in vocabulary as sources change but similarity in content. Patience is a frequent demand in scripture, e.g., Rom. 12:1–21; Heb. 6:12, 15; 10:32–39; 12:1–24; 1 Pet. 4:12–19; Rev. 13:10; 14:12. The Christian is not called to destroy the world, but to endure its attacks and overcome it by the power of the Spirit. See further U. Falkenroth and C. Brown, "Patience," *NIDNTT*, vol. 2, pp. 768–76.

Until the Lord's coming has sometimes been seen as God's coming, as in 1 Enoch 92–105. However, by the time of James the term *parousia* had become a technical term for Christ's coming: Matt. 24:3, 27, 37, 39; 1 Cor. 15:23; 1 Thess. 2:19; 5:23; 2 Thess. 2:1; 2 Pet. 1:16; 3:4; 1 John 2:28. Thus it would be unusual if it suddenly changed here to mean God's coming. The fact that James does also refer to God as judge in 4:1–5 is not a real problem. Those who urge this objection fail to note two things: Revelation, John, and other works refer to God as judge and then shift to speak of Christ as judge; and James 5:6 marks the end of a major section. For the various positions, see further G. Braumann, "Present," *NIDNTT*, vol. 2, pp. 898–901; M. Dibelius, *James*, pp. 242–43; S. S. Laws, *James*, pp. 208–9.

The **autumn and spring rains** are characteristic of the east end of the Mediterranean south of the Taurus Mountains. The further south one goes, the less reliable and more important these rains are. Though mentioned in the Old Testament (Deut. 11:14; Jer. 5:24; Hosea 6:3; Joel 2:24; Zech. 10:1), there is no evidence that James has a specific scriptural passage in mind. See further D. Baly, *The Geography of the Bible*, pp. 47–52.

5:8 / **Stand firm** is a translation of the idea found in Pss. 57:7; 90:17; Rom. 1:11; 1 Thess. 3:13; 2 Thess. 2:17; Heb. 13:9. The idea of internal stamina and strengthening must somehow be included, even if the more literal "strengthen" or "establish your hearts" is unacceptable in a modern English version. See further G. Harder, *Sterizō*, *TDNT*, vol. 7, pp. 655–57.

The **is near** formula occurs frequently outside the Gospels for the coming of the Lord: Rom. 13:12; Heb. 10:25; 1 Pet. 4:7. These are not so much time references as indications of immanence: "be prepared," "hold on."

5:9 / The term to **grumble** (lit. "groan") is frequently found in the Greek Old Testament in Job and the prophets. In the New Testament the creation groans (Rom. 8:23) and Christians (including Paul) groan (2 Cor. 5:2). But Christians must not make *others* groan (Heb. 13:17).

In **or you will be judged** James shows a typical use of the Jesus teaching tradition. In a similar manner in 1 Cor. 7:10, Paul takes a teaching of Jesus and applies it pastorally in two ways. First, it binds a couple *within the church* so that Paul permits no divorce. Separation may be necessary, but it can never be recognized as permanent (therefore no remarriage is allowed), for Jesus' word is authoritative. But second, when one of the partners is *outside the church* and church discipline, Paul must extend the implication of Jesus' teaching. The *Christian* must not end the marriage, but he or she is not bound if the other partner does. This illustrates the application of Jesus' teaching to a new situation. James takes Jesus' teaching in Matt. 7:1 and draws an implication in another direction. If Jesus taught that Christians should not judge, then they will be judged for the act of judging.

That **the Judge is standing at the door!** is a typical New Testament teaching with respect to both the judgment of believers (1 Cor. 3:10–17; 2 Cor. 5:10) and the imminence of judgment (Matt. 24:33, 45–51; Mark 13:29, 34–37; Luke 12:42–46; Rev. 3:3, 20). This tension is a motivation in the Christian life.

5:10 / In **take the prophets** James presents the numerous lists in canonical and extracanonical literature: 1 Macc. 2:49–64; Sirach 44–50; Jubilees; Matt. 23:29–31; Heb. 11. Other apocryphal books (e.g., the Martyrdom of Isaiah) reported tales of deaths of prophets. All of this material, along with histories (2 and 4 Maccabees are extensive martyrologies), played the same role that *Foxe's Book of Martyrs* or *The Martyr's Mirror* played for past generations of Christians. Significantly, James does not cite Christian martyrs, which means he is too early for a large number of such stories to exist.

5:11 / The **blessed**ness of those who **persevered** is a key theme in scripture. The term for "persevere" here is the same one found in 1:12 and also in 4 Macc. 7:22. See further N. Becker, "Blessing," *NIDNTT*, vol. 1, pp. 215–18 and F. Hauck, "*Hypomenō*," *TDNT*, vol. 4, pp. 585–88. Job is mentioned in *Testament of Abraham* 15:10 and 1 Clement 17 as an example, but the full extent of the tradition appears in the Greek Testament of Job, which James may never have seen but which contains oral traditions he surely knew. The whole Testament revolves around patient endurance. The Testament also underlines Job's charity (cf. Job 29:12–17; 31:16–23) and stresses his sufferings as a test from Satan, similar to the tradition of the testing of Abraham. Thus the allusion to Job catches up the theme of James 2. See further P. H. Davids, "Tradition and Citation in the Epistle of James."

The phrase for **what the Lord finally brought about** is simply, "the end of the Lord." Some believe this end refers to the coming of Christ, others that the end refers to the results of Christ's sufferings. In both these cases **Lord** must mean "Christ." Most likely, however, in the context of Job, **Lord** means "God" and the end is how God cared for Job in Job 42.

The term **full of compassion** is found in the New Testament only here. It is an intensive term created by the early church to express God's compassion (cf. Rom 8:28ff.). The term is stronger than the word used in the Greek Old Testament in the Psalms (103:8; 111:4). It occurs later in Hermas (*Vision* 1.3.2; 2.2.8; 4.2.3; *Mandate* 4.3.5; 9.2) and other early Christian literature.

5:12 / Though the Old Testament regulates **swear**ing and oaths (Lev. 19:12; Num. 30:3) and God swears oaths (Num. 14:21; Deut. 4:31; 7:8), they were a constant problem during the Old Testament period (Jer. 7:9; Hos. 4:2; Zech. 5:3–4; Mal. 3:5). The Greeks had similar problems. In the Dead Sea Scrolls almost all oaths were prohibited. Paul still uses oaths in the New Testament (Rom. 1:9; Gal. 1:20; 2 Cor. 1:23; 11:11; Phil. 1:8; 1 Thess. 2:5, 10), although he uses them, not to imply he might not be speaking truth elsewhere, but to state that no matter how unbelievable his point might seem God knew it was true. Paul is so far from having two levels of truthfulness in language that in 2 Cor. 1:5–2:4 he defends himself for changing travel plans. Once he announced the plans he was bound by them unless other, then unknown, weighty matters came up later.

Jesus' saying in the Greek text and in some translations has a doubled **Yes**, and **No**. Some argue that this is a substitute oath; "yes, yes" is a firm promise, "yes" is not. But the NIV correctly understands Matt. 5:34–37, for in Jewish parallels the "yes-yes" formula means that one's outer "yes" should match an inner-heart "yes," i.e., there should be absolute truthfulness and no hypocrisy. James' verbal differences from Matthew simply show that he has a variant version of the oral tradition.

See further S. S. Laws, *James*, pp. 219–24; H. G. Link, "Swear," *NIDNTT*, vol. 3, pp. 737–43; P. Minear, "Yes or No, the Demand for Honesty in the Early Church"; J. Schneider, "*Omnyō*," *TDNT*, vol. 5, pp. 176–85; and "*Horkos*," *TDNT*, vol. 5, pp. 459–61.

5:13 / The word for **trouble** refers to the inner experience of misfortune or misadventure. For example, Josephus uses it for military reverses. See further W. Michaelis, "*Kakopatheō*," *TDNT*, vol. 5, pp. 936–37.

Sing songs of praise is used fifty-six times in the Greek Old Testament, originally meaning a song with string accompaniment (Pss. 33:2, 3; 98:4, 5; 147:7; 149:3). Later it meant any song of praise (Pss. 7:17; 9:2). In the New Testament one might sing praises in painful circumstances (Acts 5:41; 16:25) as well as in more comfortable circumstances (1 Cor. 14:15). Songs might be Old Testament psalms, traditional hymns (e.g., 1 Tim. 3:16), or improvised (1 Cor. 14:15; Eph. 5:19–20). The important thing was to be constantly thankful to God for whatever blessings one had (Phil. 4:4, 6; 1 Thess. 5:16–18).

5:14 / On the differential attitude towards suffering and sickness in the New Testament see P. H. Davids, "Suffering and Illness in the New Testament," in *Understanding Power Evangelism* (forthcoming; title tentative), eds. Douglas Pennoyer and C. Peter Wagner (Ventura, Calif.: Regal Books, 1989).

Both Old Testament Judaism (Exod. 3:16; Ezra 10:14) and New Testament Judaism (Matt. 26:3; cf. Susanna 5, 29, 34) were governed by elders. Each synagogue, town, and national unit had its elders. The early church borrowed this organization; hence Paul appointed elders under the inspiration of the Spirit (Acts 11:30; 14:23; 15:2; 20:17). Later writings indicate the standards for selection of elders and their proper functions (1 Tim. 3; 5:17; Titus 1:5; 1 Pet. 5:1; 2 John 1). Thus the readers of the epistle would have been very familiar with elders as the leaders of their local congregation and of the church of a citywide area (a group of house churches, none of which had more than forty to sixty members). See further G. Bornkamm, *"Presbyteros,"* TDNT, vol. 6, pp. 651–83, and L. Coenen, "Bishop," NIDNTT, vol. 1, pp. 192–201.

Praying **over him** is prayer at the bedside in the hearing of the person, probably including the laying of hands upon the person.

The **oil** (olive oil) is not the medicinal oil of Isa. 1:6 or Jer. 8:22 or other Jewish and Greek sources, although it may be related to the heavenly "oil of gladness" of the coming age (Isa. 61:3). It is an important part of the rite of healing, as water is of baptism, and thus has been retained to this day in the more formalized rites of healing of the more liturgical churches (as in the Episcopal Book of Common Prayer, pp. 455–56). In those rites, however, it runs the risk of taking on a magical power, an idea foreign to James, who never blesses the oil but simply calls upon God. See further H. Schlier, *"Aleiphō,"* TDNT, vol. 1, pp. 230–32. On healing in general see F. MacNutt, *Healing* (Notre Dame, Ind.: Ave Maria Press, 1974) and *The Power to Heal* (Notre Dame, Ind.: Ave Maria Press, 1977); and Roy Lawrence, *Christian Healing Rediscovered* (Downers Grove, Ill.: Inter-Varsity Press, 1980); even more up-to-date and practical are K. Blue, *Authority to Heal* (Downers Grove, Ill.: Inter-Varsity Press, 1987) and J. Wimber, *Power Healing* (San Francisco: Harper & Row, 1986).

The name of the Lord was named over people in baptism (Acts 8:16; 10:48; 19:5; cf. Matt. 28:19), healing, and exorcism (Mark 9:38; Luke 10:17; Acts 3:6, 16; 4:7; 9:34). It was a calling out of the name of Jesus to ask him to intervene as appropriate: initiate the candidate into his church, heal, or drive out the demon. Thus it was an act that showed it was *God's* power doing the work and at the same time opened the situation to God's power. See further H. Bietenhard, *"Onoma,"* TDNT, vol. 5, p. 277; M. Kelsey, *Healing and Christianity*, pp. 104–99; and S. S. Laws, *James*, pp. 225–32.

5:15 / The relationship of **faith** to prayer is also important for Mark 2:5; 5:34; 10:52; and Acts 14:9. The locus of faith in most Gospel miracles and many miracles in Acts is in the person who prays (normally Jesus); only rarely is the person who is healed said to have faith. Rejection of Christ prevents healing, but the amount of faith in the patient is biblically unimportant.

Scripture teaches that **sin** can cause illness, but it also teaches that not all illness is caused by sin (2 Kings 19:15–19; 20:3; Job; Mark 2:5; John 5:14; 9:2–3; 1 Cor. 11:30). Thus James uses a conditional clause: "if he may have committed sin." Total healing will include the forgiveness of sin (Matt. 12:32; Mark 2:5; Luke 12:10), so the opportunity for

examination, confession, and a declaration of forgiveness should be offered. The rabbinic advice "if a person is visited by painful sufferings,
let him examine himself" (b. *Berakoth* 5a) is still good for the Christian,
but where dutiful self-examination reveals nothing, the person should
remember Job. The rabbis also taught there were chastisements of love
(undeserved sufferings) as well as chastisements of reproof (suffering
deserved due to sin).

5:16 / The Old Testament is full of confessions. Many of the
psalms, for example, are public confessions of sin, often with a response
of forgiveness and healing. See Lev. 5:5; Num. 5:7; Job 33:26–28; Pss.
32:5; 38:3–4; 40:12; 51:2–5; Prov. 20:9; 28:13. There were also prayers of
confession for the community (Lev. 16:21; 26:40; Dan. 9:4–10). The intertestamental period continued this tradition (Psalms of Solomon 9:6; Judith 9:1–14; Tobit 3:1–6; 3 Macc. 2:2–20; 6:2–15). The Dead Sea Scrolls
prescribed confession before the community (1 QS 1:23–2:1; CD 20). All
of this forms the background to early Christianity, in which John the Baptist began with public confession (Matt. 3:6; Mark 1:5), church discipline demanded confession (Matt. 18:15–22; Gal. 6:1–3), and the
documents of the New Testament witness to it (Acts 19:18; 1 John 1:9).
In the postapostolic church, public confession of sin continued, particularly as a prelude to prayer (1 Clement 51:3; Didache 4:14; Barnabas 19:12;
Hermas *Visions* 1.1.3; 3.1.5–6; *Similitude* 9.23.4). If the later church forgot
forgiveness, became prudish in what it described as sin, and then formalized, ritualized, and individualized confession, this should not obscure
the healthiness of the early practice. Confession leads to forgiveness (for
the forgiver as well as the sinner, Matt. 6:14–15), and this leads to health
in general (1 Cor. 11:30–32; 1 John 5:16–17). This relationship between
confession, public and private; discipline; forgiveness; and health must
not be forgotten. See further M. Jeschke, *Disciplining the Brother* (Scottdale,
Penn.: Herald Press, 1979).

The **righteous** person is not a specially holy person but the community member who has confessed his or her sins and so is living in
harmony with God. In the Old Testament many people are declared righteous (Gen. 18:16–33; 20:7; Num. 21:7; Job 42:8; Jer. 15:1), but the same
is true in the New Testament (Matt. 1:19; Heb. 12:23; 1 Pet. 4:18; 1 John
3:7; Rev. 22:11). See further H. Seebass and C. Brown, "Righteousness,"
NIDNTT, vol. 3, pp. 358–77.

The final word in the verse is a participle, *energoumenē* (NIV **effective**). A study of S. S. Laws, *James*, p. 234; J. H. Ropes, *James*, p. 309;
J. B. Mayor, *James*, p. 177–79; and J. B. Adamson, *James*, p. 199, reveals
as many attempts to interpret the word as there are commentators. James
is surely not referring to how hard one prays (Laws), but more likely
to the effectiveness of prayer (Mayor).

5:17–18 / **Elijah** prays in 1 Kings 17:20–22, but that is in a story
other than the one cited. Yet by the time of 2 Esdras 7:109, he is a powerful man of prayer: "and Elijah [prayed] for those who received the rain,

and for one who was dead, that he might live." Later Jewish tradition presents him as an intercessor for Israel who occasionally returns to earth. See further P. H. Davids, "Tradition and Interpretation in the Epistle of James," pp. 119–21; and J. Jeremias, *"Elias," TDNT*, vol. 2, pp. 929–30.

The **three and a half years** (cf. Luke 4:25) are not in the Old Testament but come from tradition, perhaps as one-half of seven, the standard period of judgment (Gen. 41:25–36; Dan. 7:25; 12:7; Rev. 11:2; 12:14). Thus it is a symbolic round figure.

5:19 / On the structure of the epistle, see the Introduction and F. O. Francis, "The Form and Function of the Opening and Closing paragraphs of James and 1 John."

In the Old Testament **wander** was frequently used for serious error: Prov. 14:8; Jer. 23:17; Ezek. 33:10; 34:4. It is similarly used in the Dead Sea Scrolls and the Testaments of the Twelve Patriarchs. This sense of a moral departure from the faith (often due to demonic entrapment) also is frequent in the New Testament: Matt. 18:12–13; 24:4–5, 11; Mark 12:24; 13:5–6; Rom. 1:27; Eph. 4:14; 2 Thess. 2:11; 2 Tim. 3:13; Titus 3:3; 1 Pet. 2:25; 2 Pet. 2:15–18; 1 John 2:26; 4:6; Rev. 2:20. The early church took most seriously a consistent moral departure from its standards, whether over money, speech (gossip), food (gluttony, intoxication), anger, or sex. These were all grounds for excommunication. See further M. Jeschke, *Disciplining the Brother*; and W. Gunther, "Lead Astray," *NIDNTT*, vol. 2, pp. 457–61.

Truth was a way to live in Judaism (Pss. 25:4–5; 26:3; 86:11), as it is in the New Testament (Matt. 22:16; John 3:21; 14:6; Rom. 1:18; Eph. 6:14; 1 Pet. 1:22; 1 John 1:6). This is clear in 1 John where the phrase "doing the truth" occurs. The truth is not so much believed as acted upon.

To **bring him back** is literally "to cause him to turn around." It is an "about-face," which is the way scripture usually pictures repentance (Isa. 6:10; Ezek. 33:11; Acts 3:19; 9:35; 2 Cor. 3:16). The person must be brought to recognize the error of the wrong way of life, to reject that life, and to reverse course and begin following the correct way of life. People are encouraged to help in this process from Leviticus (19:17) to Jude (23). See further Ps. 51:13; Ezek. 3:17–21; 33:7–9; 1 Thess. 5:14; 2 Thess. 3:15; 2 Tim. 2:25; 1 John 5:16; and F. Laubach, "Conversion," *NIDNTT*, vol. 1, pp. 353–55.

5:20 / The idea of **death** as the penalty for sin is usually that of eternal judgment: Deut. 30:19; Job 8:13; Pss. 1:6; 2:12; Prov. 2:18; 14:12; Jer. 23:12. The soul is not a part of the person, but the whole person, physical and spiritual. See further C. Brown, "Soul," *NIDNTT*, vol. 3, pp. 676–89; W. Schmithals, "Death," *NIDNTT*, vol. 1, pp. 430–41.

The **covering over a multitude of sins** means to forgive, pictured as cultic atonement (i.e., sins are covered by sacrificial blood): Pss. 32:1; 85:2; Dan. 4:24; Rom. 4:7. The **multitude of sins** is not to stress the wickedness of the sinner but the extent of God's grace (Ps. 85:2, Ezek. 28:17). A related expression from Prov. 10:12, "Love covers over all wrongs" or "Love covers a multitude of sins," is quoted in 1 Pet. 4:8. It became a favorite of the church fathers, who believed Jesus coined James' version of the saying.

The one problematic issue in this verse is whether the action will save **him** [that sinner] or **him** [the rescuer]. The Greek is not clear, but the NIV has probably made the correct choice. There is a scriptural tradition that places responsibility on the rescuer (Ezek. 3:18–21; 33:9; 1 Tim. 4:16); to callously watch someone go to his or her death spiritually (and often physically as well) without trying to warn that person is to endanger your own soul, for now you are the one outside of the way of Jesus, who never failed to warn and save people. This may not be James' meaning (although M. Dibelius, *James*, pp. 258–60, and S. S. Laws, *James*, pp. 240–41, believe it is), but it is in scripture and may well have motivated him to do the act of warning and rescue that is his Epistle.

For Further Reading

Commentaries on James

Adamson, J. B. *The Epistle of James*. NICNT, Grand Rapids: Wm. B. Eerdmans, 1976.

Alford, H. *The Greek Testament*. London: Rivingtons, 1859.

Barclay, W. *The Letters of James and Peter*. Philadelphia: Westminster, 1961

Bennett, W. H. *The General Epistles*. The Century Bible. Edinburgh: T. C. and E. C. Jack, 1901.

Blackman, E. C. *The Epistle of James*. Torch Bible Commentaries. London: SCM Press, 1957.

Bowman, J. W. *The Letter of James*. The Layman's Bible Commentary 24. Richmond: John Knox Press, 1962.

Burdick, D. W. *James*. Expositor's Bible Commentary. Vol. 12. Ed. F. E. Gaebelein. Grand Rapids: Zondervan, 1981.

Cadoux, A. T. *The Thought of St. James*. London: J. Clark & Co., 1944.

Carpenter, W. B. *The Wisdom of James the Just*. London: Isbister and Co., 1903.

Carr, A. *The General Epistle of St. James*. Cambridge Greek Testament for Schools and Colleges. Cambridge: Cambridge University Press, 1899.

Dale, R. W. *The Epistle of James*. London: Hodder & Stoughton, 1895.

Davids, P. H. *The Epistle of James*. NIGTC. Grand Rapids: Wm. B. Eerdmans, 1982.

Dibelius, M. *James*: Hermeneia. Philadelphia: Fortress Press, 1976.

Easton, B. S. *The Epistle of James*. The Interpreter's Bible. Vol. 12. New York: Abingdon Press, 1957.

Fickett, H. L., Jr. *James: Faith That Works*. Glendale, Calif.: Regal Books, 1972.

Hiebert, D. E. *The Epistle of James: Tests of a Living Faith*. Chicago: Moody Press, 1979.

Hort, F. J. A. *The Epistle of St. James*. London: Macmillan & Co., 1909.

Hubbard, D. A. *The Book of James: Wisdom that Works.* Waco: Word Books, 1980.

Huther, J. E. *Critical and Exegetical Handbook to the General Epistles of James and John.* Edinburgh: T. & T. Clark, 1882.

Jones, R. B. *The Epistles of James, John, and Jude.* Grand Rapids: Baker Book House, 1961.

Kelly, E. *James: A Primer for Christian Living.* Nutley, N.J.: The Craig Press, 1969.

King, G. H. *A Belief that Behaves.* Fort Washington, Penn.: Christian Literature Crusade, 1941.

Kistemaker, S. J. *The New Testament Commentary: Exposition of the Epistle of James and the Epistles of John.* Grand Rapids: Baker Book House, 1986.

Knowling, R. J. *The Epistle of St. James.* London: Methuen & Co., 1904.

Kugelman, R. *James and Jude.* The New Testament Message. Vol. 19. Wilmington: M. Glazier; Dublin: Veritas, 1980.

Laws, S. S. *A Commentary on the Epistle of James.* HNTC. San Francisco: Harper & Row, 1980.

Martin, R. A. *James.* Augsburg Commentary on the New Testament. Minneapolis: Augsburg, 1982.

Martin, R. P. *James.* Word Biblical Commentary. Vol. 48. Waco: Word Books, 1988.

Mayor, J. B. *The Epistle of St. James.* 3rd ed. London: Macmillan & Co., 1910.

Mitton, C. L. *The Epistle of James.* London: Marshall, Morgan & Scott, 1966.

Moffatt, J. *The General Epistles.* MNTC. London: Hodder & Stoughton, 1928.

Moo, D. *James.* Tyndale New Testament Commentary, revised. Grand Rapids: Wm. B. Eerdmans, 1987.

Motyer, J. A. *The Tests of Faith.* London: Inter-Varsity Press, 1970.

_____. *The Message of James.* The Bible Speaks Today. Leicester/Downers Grove, Ill.: Inter-Varsity Press, 1985.

Oesterley, W. E. *The General Epistle of James.* The Expositor's Greek Testament. Vol. 4. London: Hodder & Stoughton, 1910.

Parry, R. St. J. *A Discussion of the General Epistle of St. James.* London: C. J. Clay & Sons, 1903.

Plummer, A. *The General Epistles of St. James and St. Jude.* The Expositor's Bible. London: Hodder & Stoughton, 1891.

Plumptre, E. H. *The General Epistle of St. James.* Cambridge Bible for Schools and Colleges. Cambridge: Cambridge University Press, 1876.

Reicke, B. I. *The Epistles of James, Peter and Jude.* AB. Garden City, N.Y.: Doubleday, 1964.

Rendall, G. H. *The Epistle of St. James and Judaic Christianity.* Cambridge: Cambridge University Press, 1927.

Roper, D. H. *The Law That Sets You Free!* Waco, Tex.: Word Books, 1977.

Ropes, J.H. *A Critical and Exegetical Commentary on the Epistle of St. James.* ICC. Edinburgh: T. & T. Clark, 1916.

Ross, A. *The Epistles of James and John.* NICNT. Grand Rapids: Wm. B. Eerdmans, 1967.

Scaer, D. P. *James, the Apostle of Faith: A Primary Christological Document for the Persecuted Church.* St. Louis: Concordia, 1983.

Shifflett, A. *Blue Jeans Theology of James.* Cincinnati, Ohio: Standard Publishing Co. 1975.

Sidebottom, E. M. *James, Jude and 2 Peter.* The Century Bible. London: Thomas Nelson & Sons, 1967.

Smith, H. M. *The Epistle of St. James.* Oxford: Oxford University Press, 1914.

Strauss, L. *James Your Brother.* Neptune, N.J. 1956.

Stevenson, H. F. *James Speaks for Today.* London: Marshall, Morgan & Scott, 1966.

Sumner, J. B. *Practical Exposition of the General Epistles of James, Peter, John, and Jude.* London, 1840.

Tasker, R. V. G. *The General Epistle of James.* TNTC. London: Tyndale Press, 1956.

Wessel, W. W. "James, Epistle of." ISBE (1982). Vol. 2, pp. 959–66.

Williams, R. R. *The Letters of John and James.* The Cambridge Bible Commentary. Cambridge: Cambridge University Press, 1965.

Wolf, R. *The General Epistles of James and Jude.* Wheaton, Ill.: Tyndale House, 1969.

Zohiates, S. *The Behavior of Belief.* Grand Rapids: Wm. B. Eerdmans, 1959.

Related Works

Argyle, A. W. "Greek Among Palestinian Jews in New Testament Times." *NTS* 20 (1973), pp. 87–89.

Bacon, B. W. "James, Epistle of." *Encyclopaedia Britannica*. 11th ed. Vol. 15, pp. 145–46.

Baird, W. R., Jr. "Among the Mature." *Int* 13 (1959), pp. 425–32.

Baker, W. R. "Personal Speech-Ethics: A Study of the Epistle of James against its Background." Unpublished Ph.D. dissertation, University of Aberdeen, 1986.

Baly, D. *The Geography of the Bible*. New York: Harper & Row, 1974.

Baron, S. W. *A Social and Religious History of the Jews*. 2nd ed. New York. Columbia University Press,1952.

Barrett, C. K. *A Commentary on the First Epistle to the Corinthians*. HNTC. London: A. & C. Black, 1968.

Batley, J. Y. *The Problem of Suffering in the Old Testament*. Cambridge: Deighton, Bell & Co., 1916.

Best, E. "Recent Foreign New Testament Literature." *ExT* 96 (1985), pp. 329–33.Bishop E. F. F. *Apostles of Palestine*. London: Lutterworth Press, 1958.

Blue, K. *Authority to Heal*. Downers Grove, Ill.: Inter-Varsity, 1987.

Bornkamm, G. *Jesus of Nazareth*. London: Hodder & Stoughton, 1960.

Bornkamm, G., G. Barth, and H. J. Held. *Tradition and Interpretation in Matthew*. Philadelphia: Westminster Press, 1963.

Bousset, W. *Kyrios Christos*. Nashville: Abingdon Press, 1970.

Boyle, M. O. "The Stoic Paradox of James 2:10." *NTS* 31 (1985), pp. 611–17.

Brooks, J. A. "The Place of James in the New Testament." *SWJT* 12 (1969), pp. 41–55.

Brown, S. *Apostasy and Perseverance in the Theology of Luke*. AnBib 36. Rome: Pontifical Biblical Institute, 1969.

Bruce, F. F. "The General Letters." In *A New Testament Commentary*, edited by G. C. D. Howley. London: Pickering and Inglis, 1969.

Büchler, A. *The Economic Conditions in Judea after the Destruction of the Second Temple*. London: Jew's College, 1912.

Bultmann, R. *Theology of the New Testament*. 2 vols. London: SCM Press, 1952, 1955.

Burge, G. M. " 'And Threw Them Thus on Paper': Recovering the Poetic Form of James 2:14–26." *StBTh* 7 (1977), pp. 31–45.

Burkitt, F. C. *Christian Beginnings*. London: University of London Press, 1924.

_____. "The Hebrew Papyrus of the Ten Commandments." *JQR* 15 (1903), pp. 392–408.

Burton, E. D. *Spirit, Soul, and Flesh*. Chicago: University of Chicago Press, 1918.

Cadbury H. J. "The Single Eye." *HTR* 47 (1954), pp. 69–74.

Carr, A. "The Meaning of Ὁ ΚΟΣΜΟΣ in James iii, 6." *Ex* 7th ser., vol. 8 (1909), pp. 318–25.

Carroll, K. L. "The Place of James in the Early Church." *BJRL* 44 (1961), pp. 49–67.

Chadwick, H. "Justification by Faith and Hospitality." *SP* 4 pt. 2 = TU 79 (1961), p. 281.

Clark, K. W. "The Meaning of ᾽ΕΝΕΡΓΕΩ and ΚΑΤΑΡΤΕΩ in the New Testament." *JBL* 54 (1935), pp. 93–101.

Clifford, A. C. "The Gospel and Justification." *EQ* 57 (1985) 247–67.

Cooper R. M. "Prayer: A Study in Matthew and James." *Encounter* 29 (1968), pp. 268–77.

Cranfield, C. E. B. "The Message of James." *SJT* 18 (1965), pp. 182–93, 338–45.

Crenshaw, J. L. "Popular Questioning of the Justice of God in Ancient Israel." *ZAW* 82 (1970), pp. 380–95.

Cronbach, A. "The Social Ideas of the Apocrypha and the Pseudepigrapha." *HUCA* 18 (1944), pp. 119–56.

Cullmann, O. *Christ and Time*. Philadelphia: Westminster Press, 1951.

Dalman, G. H. *Jesus-Jeshua*. London: S.P.C.K., 1929.

Daube, D. *The New Testament and Rabbinic Judaism*. London: Athlone Press, 1956.

Davids, P. H. "The Epistle of James in Modern Discussion." In W. Hasase and H. Temporini, eds. *Aufstieg und Niedergang der römischen Welt*, Vol. 25,5. Berlin: Walter De Gruyter, 1988, pp. 3621–3645,

_____. "James and Jesus." In D. Wenham, ed. *Gospel Perspectives*, Vol. 5: *The Jesus Tradition Outside the Gospels*. Sheffield: JSOT Press, 1985, pp. 63–84.

_____. "The Poor Man's Gospel." *TH* 1 (1976), pp. 37–41.

_____. "Suffering and Illness in the New Testament." In *Understanding Power Evangelism* (forthcoming; title tentative), eds. D. Pennoyer and C. P. Wagner (Ventura, Calif.: Regal Books, 1989).

_____. "Tradition and Citation in the Epistle of James." In *Scripture, Tradition, and Interpretation*, edited by W. W. Gasque and W. S. LaSor, pp. 113–26. Grand Rapids: Wm. B. Eerdmans, 1978.

Davies, W. D. " 'Knowledge' in the Dead Sea Scrolls and Matthew 11:25–30." *HTR* 46 (1953), pp. 113–39.

_____. *Paul and Rabbinic Judaism*. London: S.P.C.K., 1962.

_____. *The Setting of the Sermon on the Mount*. Cambridge: Cambridge University Press, 1964.

_____. *Torah in the Messianic Age and/or the Age to Come*. Philadelphia: Fortress Press, 1952.

Deasley, A. R. G. "The Idea of Perfection in the Qumran Texts." Ph.D. thesis, Manchester, 1972.

Deissmann, A. *Light from the Ancient East*. Grand Rapids: Baker Book House, 1927, 1978.

de Vaux, R. *Ancient Israel: Its Life and Institutions*. London: Darton, Longman & Todd, 1973.

Dockery, D. S. "Commenting on Commentaries on the Book of James." *Chriswell Th. R.* 1 (1986) 167–169.

Downing, F. G. "Cynics and Christians." *NTS* 30 (1984), pp. 584–93.

Drane, J. W. *Paul: Libertine or Legalist?* London: S.P.C.K., 1975.

Du Plessis, P.-J. ΤΕΛΕΙΟΣ: *The Idea of Perfection in the New Testament*. Kampen: J. H. Kok, 1959.

Dyrness, W. "Mercy Triumphs over Justice: James 2:13 and the Theology of Faith and Works." *Themelios* 6 (1981), pp. 11–16.

Easton, B. S. "New Testament Ethical Lists." *JBL* 51 (1932), pp. 1–12.

Eckstrom, J. O. "The Discourse Structure of the Book of James." Paper, International Linguistics Center, Dallas, Texas.

Eichrodt, W. *Theology of the Old Testament*. 2 vols. London: SCM Press, 1964, 1967.

Elliott-Binns, L. E. *Galilean Christianity*. SBT 16. London: SCM Press, 1956.

_____. "James I. 18: Creation or Redemption?" *NTS* 3 (1956), pp. 148–61.

_____. "James i. 21 and Ezekiel xvi. 36: An Odd Coincidence." *ExpTim* 66 (1955), p. 273.

_____. "The Meaning of ὕλη in Jas. III. 5." *NTS* 2 (1955), pp. 48–50.

Ellis, E. E. "Wisdom and Knowledge in 1 Corinthians." In *Prophecy and Hermeneutic in Early Christianity*, pp. 45–62. Tübingen: J. C. B. Mohr, 1978. Or *Tyn.B.* 25 (1974), pp. 82–98.

Exler, F. X. J. *The Form of the Ancient Greek Letter.* Chicago: Ares, 1976.

Findlay, J. A. "James iv. 5,6." *ExpTim* 37 (1926), pp. 381–82.

Flusser, D. "Qumran and Jewish 'Apotropaic' Prayers." *IEJ* 16 (1966), pp. 194–205.

Forbes, P. B. R. "The Structure of the Epistle of James." *EvQ* 44 (1972), pp. 147–53.

Francis, F. O. "The Form and Function of the Opening and Closing Paragraphs of James and I John." *ZNW* 61 (1970), pp. 110–26.

Gerhardsson, B. *The Testing of God's Son.* ConB 2. Lund: C. W. K. Gleerup, 1966.

Gertner, M. "Midrashic Terms and Techniques in the New Testament: The Epistle of James, a Midrash on a Psalm." *SE* 3 (1964), p. 463 = TU 88.

_____. "Midrashim in the New Testament." *JSS* 7 (1962), pp. 267–92, 283–91.

Ginzberg, L. *The Legends of the Jews.* Philadelphia: Jewish Publication Society, 1913.

Godet, F. *Studies in the New Testament.* London: Hodder & Stoughton, 1876.

Goodenough, E. R. *Jewish Symbols in the Greco-Roman Period.* New York: Pantheon Books, 1953.

Goodspeed, E. J. *An Introduction to the New Testament.* Chicago: University of Chicago Press, 1937.

Gordon, R. P. "καὶ τὸ τέλος τοῦ κυρίου εἴδετε (James 5, 11)." *JTS* 26 (1975), pp. 91–95.

Gowan, D. E. "Wisdom and Endurance in James." Paper read to the 1980 meeting of the Eastern Great Lakes Biblical Society, Pittsburgh.

Grant, F. C. *The Economic Background of the Gospels.* Oxford: Oxford University Press, 1926.

Guillaume. A. "The Midrash in the Gospels." *ExpTim* 37 (1926), p. 394.

Guthrie, D. "The Development of the Idea of Canonical Pseudepigrapha in New Testament Criticism." *VE* 1 (1962), pp. 4–59.

_____. *New Testament Introduction*. 3rd ed. Downers Grove, Ill.: Inter-Varsity Press, 1970.

Hadidian, D. Y. "Palestinian Pictures in the Epistle of James." *ExpTim* 63 (1952), pp. 227–28.

Halston, B. R. "The Epistle of James: 'Christian Wisdom'?" *SE* (1968), pp. 308–14 = TU 102.

Hamann, H. P. "Faith and Works in Paul and James." *Lutheran Theological Journal* 9 (1975), pp. 33–41.

Hatch, W. H. P. "Note on the Hexameter in James 1:17." *JBL* 28 (1909), pp. 149–51.

Heichelheim, F. M. "Roman Syria." In *An Economic Survey of Ancient Rome*, edited by T. Frank, vol. 4, pp. 121–257. Baltimore: Johns Hopkins Press, 1933–1940.

Henderlite, "The Epistle of James." *Int* 3 (1949), pp. 460–76.

Hengel, M. *Property and Riches in the Early Church*. Philadelphia: Fortress Press, 1974.

Hiebert, D. E. "The Unifying Themes of the Epistle of James." *Bibliotheca Sacra* 125 (1978), pp. 221–231.

Hiers, R. H. "Friends by Unrighteous Mammon." *JAAR* 38 (1970), pp. 30–36.

Hill, R. "An Analysis of James 3–5 to the Paragraph Constituent Level." Paper, 1978, International Linguistics Center, Dallas, Tex.

Honeycutt, R. L. "James." *RevEx* 83 (1986), pp. 355–438.

Jacob, I. "The Midrashic Background for James II, 21–23." *NTS* 22 (1975), pp. 457–64.

Jeremias, J. *Jerusalem in the Time of Jesus*. London: SCM Press, 1969.

_____. *The Prayers of Jesus*. SBT ser. 2, no. 6. London: SCM Press, 1967.

Jocelyn, H. D. "*Horace*, Epistles 1." *Liverpool Classical Monthly* 4 (1979), pp. 145–46.

Jocz, J. "God's 'Poor' People." *Judaica* 28 (1972), pp. 7–29.

Johanson, B. C. "The Definition of 'Pure Religion' in James 1:27 Reconsidered" *ExpTim* 84 (1973), pp. 118–19.

Jones, P. R. "Approaches to the Study of the Book of James." *RevExp* 66 (1969), pp. 425–34.

Keck, L. E. "The Poor Among the Saints in the New Testament," *ZNW* 56 (1965), pp. 100–129.

Kelsey, M. *Healing and Christianity*, New York: Harper & Row, 1973.

Kennedy, H. A. A. "The Hellenistic Atmosphere of the Epistle of James." *Ex* ser. 8, no. 2 (1911), pp. 37–52.

Kidd, B. J. *Documents Illustrative of the History of the Church*. London: S.P.C.K., 1923.

Kirk, J. A. "The Meaning of Wisdom in James." *NTS* 16 (1969), pp. 24–38.

Kilmartin, E. J. "The Interpretation of James 5:14–15 in the Armenian Catena on the Catholic Epistles: Scholium 82." *Orient Chr. Per.* 53 (1987), pp. 335–64.

Kistemaker, S. J. "The Theological Message of James." *JETS* 29 (1986), pp. 55–61.

Klausner, J. *Jesus of Nazareth*. London: George Allen & Unwin, 1925.

Knox, W. L. "The Epistle of St. James." *JTS* 46 (1945), pp. 10–17.

Kümmel, W. G. *Introduction to the New Testament*. London: SCM Press, 1966.

Laws, S. S. "Does Scripture Speak in Vain?" *NTS* 20 (1974), pp. 210–15. Cf. S. S. C. Marshall.

Leaney, A. R. C. "Eschatological Significance of Human Suffering in the Old Testament and the Dead Sea Scrolls," *SJT* 16 (1963), pp. 286–96.

Lightfoot, J. B. *Saint Paul's Epistle to the Galatians*. London: Macmillan and Co., 1896.

Lindblom, J. "Wisdom in the Old Testament Prophets." In *Wisdom in Israel and in the Ancient Near East* (*Fest.* H. H. Rowley), *VTSup* 3, edited by M. Noth and D. W. Thomas, pp. 192–204. Leiden: E. J. Brill, 1955.

Lodge, J. G. "James and Paul at Cross-purposes?" *Bib* 62 (1981), pp. 195–213.

Lohmeyer, E. *The Lord's Prayer*. London: Collins, 1965.

Longenecker, R. N. *Biblical Exegesis in the Apostolic Period*. Grand Rapids: Wm. B. Eerdmans, 1975.

_____. *Paul, Apostle of Liberty*. Grand Rapids: Baker Book House, 1976.

Lorenzen, T. "Faith without Works Does Not Count before God! James 2:14–26." *ExpTim* 89 (1978), pp. 231–35.

Luff, S. G. A. "The Sacrament of the Sick." *Clergy Review* 52 (1967), pp. 56–60.

MacGorman, J. W. "Introducing the Book of James." *SWJT* 12 (1969), pp. 9–22.

McNeile, A. H. *Introduction to the Study of the New Testament*, 2nd ed. Oxford: Oxford University Press, 1953.

Malina, B. J. "Some Observations on the Origin of Sin in Judaism and St. Paul." *CBQ* 31 (1969), pp. 18–34.

Manson, T. W. "The Lord's Prayer." *BJRL* 38 (1955), pp. 99–113, 436–48.

Marmorstein, A. "The Background of the Haggadah." *HUCA* 6 (1926), pp. 141–204. Or *Studies in Jewish Theology*. Oxford: Oxford University Press, 1950.

_____. *The Doctrine of Merits in Old Rabbinic Literature*. New York: Ktav, 1968.

Marshall, S. S. C. "Δίψυχος: A Local Term?" *SE* 6 (1969), pp. 348–51 = TU 112 (1973).

Martin, R. P. "The Life-Setting of the Epistle of James in the Light of Jewish History." In *Biblical and Near Eastern Studies (Fest. W. S. LaSor)*, edited by G. A. Tuttle, pp. 97–103. Grand Rapids: Wm. B. Eerdmans, 1978.

_____. *New Testament Foundations*. Grand Rapids: Wm. B. Eerdmans, 1978.

Maston T. B. "Ethical Dimensions of James." *SWJT* 12 (1969), pp. 23–39.

Matthews, K. A., and Dockery, D. S., eds. *James. Chriswell Th. R.* 1 (1986), pp. 3–170.

Maynard-Reid, P. U. *Poverty and Wealth in James*. Maryknoll, N.Y.: Orbis Books, 1987.

Meecham, H. G. "The Epistle of James." *ExpTim* 49 (1937), pp. 181–83.

Minear, P. S. "Yes or No, The Demand for Honesty in the Early Church." *NovT* 13 (1971), pp. 1–13.

Miranda, J. *Marx and the Bible*. Maryknoll: Orbis Books, N.Y., 1974.

Moore, G. F. *Judaism in the First Centuries of the Christian Era*. 2 vols. Cambridge: Harvard University Press, 1950.

Moule, C. F. D. *An Idiom Book of New Testament Greek*. Cambridge: Cambridge University Press, 1968.

Moulton, J. H. "The Epistle of James and the Sayings of Jesus." *Ex* ser. 7, no. 4 (1907), pp. 45–55.

Murphy, R. E. "Yēser in the Qumran Literature." *Bib* 39 (1958), pp. 334–44.

Navone, J. *Themes of St. Luke*. Rome: Gregorian University Press, 1970.

O'Callaghan, J. "New Testament Papyri in Qumrān Cave 7?" Sup. to *JBL* 91 (1972), pp. 1–14.

Peake, A. S. *The Problem of Suffering in the Old Testament*. London: Robert Bryant, 1904.

Perdue, L. G. "Paraenesis and the Epistle of James." *ZNW* 72 (1981), pp. 241–56.

Perrin, N. *What is Redaction Criticism?* London: SCM Press, 1970.

Pichar, C. " 'Is Anyone Sick Among You?' " *CBQ* 7 (1945), pp. 165–74.

Polhill, J. B. "The Life-Situation of the Book of James." *RevExp* 66 (1969), pp. 369–78.

Porter, F. C. "The Yeçer Hara: A Study in the Jewish Doctrine of Sin." In *Biblical and Semitic Studies*, pp. 93–156. New York: Charles Scribner's Sons, 1901.

Powell, C. H. " 'Faith' in James and its Bearing on the Problem of the Date of the Epistle." *ExpTim* 62 (1950), pp. 311–14.

Prentice, W. K. "James, the Brother of the Lord." In *Studies in Roman Economic and Social History (Fest. A. C. Johnson)*, edited by P. R. Coleman-Norton, pp. 144–51. Princeton: Princeton University Press, 1951.

Rankin, O. S. *Israel's Wisdom Literature*. Edinburgh: T. & T. Clark, 1936.

Reese, J. M. "The Exegete and the Sage: Hearing the Message of James." *Biblical Theology Bulletin* 12 (1982), pp. 82–85.

Reicke, B. I. "Traces of Gnosticism in the Dead Sea Scrolls?" *NTS* 1 (1954), pp. 137–41.

Roberts, D. J. "The Definition of 'Pure Religion' in James 1:27." *ExpTim* 83 (1972), pp. 215–16.

Robertson, A. T. *A Grammar of the Greek New Testament in the Light of Historical Research*. Nashville: Broadman Press, 1934.

Rountree, C. "Further Thoughts on the Discourse Structure of James." Paper, International Linguistics Center, Dallas, Tex., 1976.

Rylaarsdam, J. C. *Revelation in Jewish Wisdom Literature*. Chicago: University of Chicago Press, 1946.

Salmon, G. *Historical Introduction to the Study of the Books of the New Testament*. 7th ed. London: John Murray, 1894.

Sanday, W. "Some Further Remarks on the Corbey St. James (ff)" *SB* 1 (1885), pp. 233–63.

Sanders, E. P. *Paul and Palestinian Judaism*. Philadelphia: Fortress Press, 1977.

Sanders, J. A. *Suffering as Divine Discipline in the Old Testament and Post-Biblical Judaism*. Rochester, N.Y.: Colgate Rochester Divinity School, 1955.

Sanders, J. T. *Ethics in the New Testament*. Philadelphia: Fortress Press, 1975.

Schechter, S. *Some Aspects of Rabbinic Theology*. London: Adam & Charles Black, 1909.

Schmithals, W. *Paul and James*. SBT 46. London: SCM Press, 1965.

Schmitt, J. J. "You Adulteresses: the Image in James 4:4." *NovT* 28 (1986), pp. 327–37.

Schnackenburg, R. *The Moral Teaching of the New Testament*. London: Burns & Oates, 1965.

Schökel, L. A. "James 5,2 and 4,6." *Bib* 54 (1973), pp. 73–76.

Schürer, E. *The History of the Jewish People in the Age of Jesus Christ*. Edinburgh: T. & T. Clark, 1973, 1979.

Seitz, O. J. F. "Afterthoughts on the Term 'Dipsychos.' " *NTS* 4 (1958), pp. 327–34.

_____. "Antecedents and Significance of the Term ΔΙΨΥΧΟΣ." *JBL* 66 (1947), pp. 211–19.

_____. "James and the Law." *SE* 2 (1964), pp. 472–86. = TU 87 (1964).

_____. "The Relationship of the Shepherd of Hermas to the Epistle of James." *JBL* 63 (1944), pp. 131–40.

_____. "Two Spirits in Man: An Essay in Biblical Exegesis." *NTS* 6 (1959), pp. 82–95.

Selwyn, E. G. *The First Epistle of St. Peter*. London: Macmillan, 1947.

Sevenster, J. N. *Do You Know Greek?* NovT Sup 19. Leiden: E. J. Brill, 1968.

Shepherd, M. H. "The Epistle of James and the Gospel of Matthew." *JBL* 75 (1956), pp. 40–51.

Smalley, S. S. "The Delay of the Parousia." *JBL* 83 (1964), pp. 41–54.

Smith, C. R. *The Bible Doctrine of Salvation*. London: Epworth Press, 1946.

Smith, G. A. *Jerusalem*. London: Hodder & Stoughton, 1907.

Smith, M. L. "James 2:8" *ExpTim* 21 (1910), p. 329.

Smyth, H. W. *Greek Grammar*. Cambridge: Harvard University Press, 1956.

Souter, A. *The Text and Canon of the New Testament*. London: Duckworth, 1913.

Stacey, W. D. *The Pauline View of Man in Relation to its Judaic and Hellenistic Background*. London: Macmillan, 1956.

Stendahl, K. *Paul among Jews and Gentiles*. Philadelphia: Fortress Press, 1976.

Sutcliffe, E. F. *Providence and Suffering in the Old and New Testaments*. London: Thomas Nelson & Sons, 1955.

Taylor, C. "St. James and Hermas." *ExpTim* 16 (1905), p. 334.

Tennant F. R. *The Sources of the Doctrine of the Fall and of Original Sin*. Cambridge: Cambridge University Press, 1903.

Thrall, M. E. *Greek Particles in the New Testament*. Grand Rapids: Wm. B. Eerdmans, 1962.

Torakawa, K. "Literary-Semantic Analysis of James 1–2." Paper, International Linguistics Center, Dallas, Tex., 1978.

Townsend, M. J. "Christ, Community and Salvation in the Epistle of James." *EvQ* 53 (1981), pp. 115–23.

_____. "James 4:1–4." *ExpTim* 87 (1975), pp. 211–13.

Trench, R. C. *Synonyms of the New Testament*. 8th ed. London: Macmillan, 1876.

Urbach, E. E. *The Sages*, Jerusalem: Magnes Press, 1975.

van Unnik, W. C. "The Teaching of Good Works in I Peter." *NTS* 1 (1954), pp. 92–110.

von Rad, G. *Old Testament Theology*. London: Oliver Boyd, 1962.

von Waldow, H. E, "Social Responsibility and Social Structure in Early Israel." *CBQ* 32 (1970), pp. 182–204.

Ward, R. B. "Partiality in the Assembly: James 2:2–4." *HTR* 62 (1969), pp. 87–97.

_____. The Works of Abraham: James 2:14–26." *HTR* 61 (1968), pp. 283–90.

Wifstrand, A. "Stylistic Problems in the Epistles of James and Peter." *ST* 1 (1948), pp. 170–82.

Williams, N. P. *The Ideas of the Fall and of Original Sin*. London: Longmans Green, 1927.

Williams, R. L. "Piety and Poverty in James." *Wesley Th J* 22 (1987), pp. 37–55.

Wimber, J. *Power Healing*. San Francisco: Harper & Row, 1986.

Wolverton, W. I. "The Double-Minded Man in the Light of the Essene Psychology." *ATR* 38 (1956), pp. 166–75.

Wordsworth, J. "The Corbey St. James (ff) and its Relation to Other Latin Versions and to the Original Language of the Epistle." *SB* 1 (1885), pp. 113–23.

Yadin, Y. *The Scroll of the War of the Sons of Light against the Sons of Darkness*. Oxford: Oxford University Press, 1962.

Yoder, J. H. *The Politics of Jesus*, Grand Rapids: Wm. B. Eerdmans, 1972.

Young, F. W. "The Relation of I Clement to the Epistle of James." *JBL* 67 (1948), pp. 339–45.

Zahn, T. *Introduction to the New Testament*. Edinburgh: T. & T. Clark, 1909.

Ziegler, J. J. "Who can anoint the sick?" *Worship* 61 (1987), pp. 25–44.

Subject Index

Aalen, S., 72
Abraham: actions proved faith of, 67–69, 77; James and Paul on, 4–5, 19, 69; monotheism of, 76–77; perseverance of, 27; Rahab compared to, 70–71; tested, 18, 44, 67–68, 77; tested by devil, 50
Account, as righteousness; *see* Credit
Action: as acceptance of word, 41–42; faith and, 19, 63–70; James vs. Paul on, 19, 69–70; peacemaking, 91, 97; salvation requires, 64; speech and, equals all behavior, 74; wisdom shown by, 87–88, 91, 97
Adamson, J. B., 54, 74, 93, 106, 135
Adulteress, desire as, 51
Adultery: murder prohibition compared with, 61; worldliness compared to, 100, 107
Aesop's crow, instability shown by, 31
Agricultural workers, exploitation of, 116, 129
Agur, 128
Akiba, Rabbi, 75
Albinus, 3
Alexander of Macedon, 81
Allen, E. L., 79
Amos, patient endurance of, 120
Anger: condemnation of, 53; control of as virtue, 39–40; of God, grace tempers, 101–2
'ani, Greek translation of, 48
Annas the Younger, 3
Antiochus IV Epiphanes, 16, 45
Apeirastos, meaning of, 50
Apocalyptic judgment, 15–16, 54; *see also* Judgment
Apostasy, unfaithfulness as, 100–101
Arnold, E., 51
Arrow and snare, image of, 51
Artisans, in Jerusalem economy, 12
Authorship, 1–7, 25, 105; date of epistle and, 9

Babylonian Talmud, on self-examination, 135
Baker, W. R., 53
Baly, D., 131
Bammel, E., 73
Baron, S. W., 127
Beck H., 94, 97
Becker, N., 132
Behavior, Christian; see Action
Belief: belief in vs. belief that, 76; faith as, 18–19, 63; as requirement for receiving, 29–30; *see also* Faith; Intellectual belief
Ben Zoma, 81
Berkhof, H., 108
Beth-din, 57
Bietenhard, H., 129, 134
Bishop, E. F. F., 95
Blessed, 34, 55, 58
Blessing: Eighteen Benedictions, 94; as result of action, 42; tongue used for, 85, 94
Blue, K., 134
Blunk, J., 55
Boasting: positive sense of, 128; as sin, 89, 113, 127–28; tongue used for, 82
Bornkamm, G., 134
Braumann, G., 131
Braun, H., 51
Breath, as spirit, 71, 79
Bring him back, 126, 136
Brothers; church members as, 31, 58; readers of letters as, 26
Brown, C., 79, 94, 97, 128, 131, 135–36
Bruce, F. F., 22
Büchsel, F., 96
Bultmann, R., 74, 76
Bunyan, J., 125
Business; of wealthy, 33–34, 111; as worldly, 112

Chadwick, H., 79

Lord and Father, 85, 94
Love your neighbor as yourself, 60
Lovelace, R., 109
Luke: beatitudes in, 16, 48–49; editing of Jesus' sayings by, 7
Luther, Martin: on authorship, 2; on Epistle of James, 1; James-Paul conflict and, 78
Luxury, 117, 129
Lycus valley, springs in, 86, 95

MacNutt, F., 134
Makarios, 49, 55
Makrothymē, hypomonē vs., 131
Malice, eliminating from heart, 54
Marah, springs in, 95
Maranthēsetai, 49
Mary, rejoicing in poverty by, 32, 48
Mastema, Abraham tested by, 50
Matthew, idea of perfection, 28, 45
Matthias, 16
Mayor, J. B., 71, 76, 95, 135
Mē, 75
Meekness, as virtue, 40–41, 96
Merchants: Christian, James on, 111; socioeconomic status of, 127
Mercy: as characteristic of wisdom, 91; charity vs., 62–63, 74; God as full of, 62, 121, 132; in judgment, 62–63
Messiah; reinterpretation of law by, 55
Meyer, R., 109
Michaelis, W., 133
Michel, O., 46, 79, 94
Minear, P., 133
Ministry, danger of, 80–81
Miranda, J., 75
Mirror, metaphor of, 41, 54–55
Misery, coming upon the rich , 114, 128
Mist, life as a, 112, 127
Mistakes; *see* Stumble,
Mitton, C. L., 76
Monotheism, Abraham as discoverer of, 68, 77
Montefiore, C. G., 75, 77
Moore, G. F., 51–52, 73, 75
Mosaic law, *see* Law, of Moses

Moses, 40
Moths have eaten, 115, 128
Mourning, as sign of repentance, 103, 109
Mundle, W., 110
Murder: discrimination against poor ·as, 61, 74, 117, 130; as metaphor for sinful acts, 99, 106; verbal abuse as, 106
Murray, A., 107
Mussner, F., 30

Necessities of life, need to provide, 64, 75
Noah, as perfect man, 45
Nomos, Paul's use of term, 78
Nonresistance, 117, 130

Oaths, prohibition on, 121–22, 133
Obedience: action based on faith as, 41, 54; blessings of, 41–42; commitment proven by, 19, 71, 78–79; judgment conquered by, 63; perfection requires, 46; *see also* Action
Oepke, A., 77, 97
Oil, in healing rites, 123, 134
Old Testament: as James' authority, 22; as law of the Kingdom, 60–61
Oppression: of poor, 59, 73, 116–17, 129–30; wealth identified with, 116, 129
Oral teachings, 21–22; epistle as, 7
Ordination, early church lacked, 80
Origen: James cited by, 9; on practice of law (Homily on Gen. 2:16), 54
Orphans; care of as piety, 43; God as father to, 55
Orthodoxy, insufficiency of, 64–70, 78, 87–88
Orthopraxis, as mark of true wisdom, 87–88
Outward appearance, prejudice based on, 57

Packer, J. I., 53
Pagan writings, on negativity of anger, 53
Paraenesis, 7
Partiality: term for, 71; warning against, 56, 60

Scripture Index